☆ ☆ ☆ ☆ ☆

# Georgia Boys with "Stonewall" Jackson

☆ ☆ ☆ ☆ ☆

☆ ☆ ☆ ☆ ☆ ☆ ☆ ☆

# Georgia Boys with "Stonewall" Jackson

## James Thomas Thompson and the Walton Infantry

☆ ☆ ☆ ☆ ☆ ☆ ☆ ☆

By
AURELIA AUSTIN

☆ ☆ ☆ ☆ ☆

UNIVERSITY OF GEORGIA PRESS
ATHENS

*In memory of*
MARY JANE THOMPSON WELLS
*who preserved the
letters of her older brother,
James Thomas Thompson*

© 1967 by the University of Georgia Press
Athens, Georgia 30602
www.ugapress.org
All rights reserved
Printed digitally in the United States of America

The Library of Congress has cataloged the hardcover edition of this book as follows:
Library of Congress Cataloging-in-Publication Data

LCCN Permalink: http://lccn.loc.gov/67031515
Austin, Aurelia.
Georgia boys with "Stonewall" Jackson; James Thomas Thompson and the Walton Infantry.
xii, 99 p. ports. 22 cm.
Based chiefly on the letters of J. T. Thompson.
Bibliographical references included in "Notes" (p. 90–93)
1. Georgia Infantry. 11th regt., 1861–1863. 2. United States—History—Civil War, 1861–1865—Regimental histories. 3. United States—History—Civil War, 1861–1865—Personal narratives, Confederate. I. Thompson, James Thomas, d. 1862.
E559.5 11th    1967
67-31515

Paperback reissue 2010 ISBN-13: 978-0-8203-3523-0
ISBN-10: 0-8203-3523-1

## Contents

☆ ☆ ☆ ☆ ☆ ☆ ☆ ☆ ☆ ☆

| | |
|---|---|
| Foreword *by Bell Irvin Wiley* | vii |
| Preface | ix |
| I "All I Want Is a Crack at a Yankey Boy" | 1 |
| II "I Dreamp That God Was Sleaping with Mee" | 8 |
| III "I Enjoy Camp Life Better Than Anybody Els I Recon" | 20 |
| IV "We Ar Station in 16 Miles of Richmond" | 31 |
| V "You Must Call Them the Malvin Hill Turnip" | 42 |
| VI "You Wanted to Know If I Am Under 'Stone Wall' or Not. I Am." | 54 |
| VII "We Lost One of Our Best Generals—That Matchless Stonewall Jackson" | 59 |
| Appendix: Muster Roll, Walton Infantry | 76 |
| Notes | 90 |
| Index | 94 |

# Illustrations

*Following page 4*

Brothers of James Thomas Thompson

General Thomas Jonathan "Stonewall" Jackson

Captain Matthew Talbot Nunnally

Brigadier General George Thomas "Tige" Anderson

Henry D. McDaniel

General James Longstreet

# Foreword

MOST of the writing about the Civil War has been focused on the generals, the armies, and the battles. The common soldiers, the small units, and the daily routine in camp have been treated as if they were of little moment. Yet the war was fought mainly by ordinary folk, and what the participants did between battles was of far greater concern to them and occupied far more of their time than fighting and skirmishing.

Aurelia Austin's book derives its importance and appeal from the fact that it tells the story of the war largely in terms of Private James Thompson and the company in which he served. It treats only incidentally the battles and dwells at length on such details of daily life as food, clothing, shelter, health, morale, discipline, and marching. It throws valuable light on the character and thought patterns of a country boy from the deep South.

James Thompson is an interesting and lovable individual. He is a fascinating combination of naiveté and shrewdness, modesty and pride, and gentleness and toughness. He recognized and responded to good leadership. He was perceptive and disdainful of incompetence in his superiors. His most impressive attributes were his patriotism and his religion. He was so thoroughly devoted to the Confederacy that no hardship or danger, however great, could depress his spirit; and once he had committed his soul to God, his faith was as unwavering as his morale. His adaptability and trust found simple but eloquent expression in the letter that he wrote his family March 26, 1862: "My Cotrig Box makes a soft pillow, the Mother Earth makes a easy bed, the heavens makes a good shelter, the Lord is a Good Genral. You must think when you lie down that our Saviour Had nowhir to lay His head. Trust in God and alls well."

The insight provided by Aurelia Austin into the experiences and reactions of this admirable young soldier reduces the war to human terms and makes it more meaningful to people of our time.

BELL IRVIN WILEY

*History Department*
*Emory University*

# Preface

"SINCE the third day of July, Eighteen Hundred & Sixty-one I have seen, heard and experienced such things I never thought I should witness," wrote Captain Matthew Talbot Nunnally of Company H to his sister Mary.

At the outbreak of the war Matthew Nunnally was a cadet at West Point Military Academy. He left the Academy and hurried home to Walton County, Georgia, where he enlisted with his friends and neighbors in the Walton Infantry as a first lieutenant.[1] The 11th Regiment, Georgia Volunteers, of which the Walton Infantry was to be known as Company H, was mustered into service in Atlanta, Georgia, on July 3, 1861.

On reaching Atlanta each of the officers in Company H was promoted. Matthew Talbot Nunnally became captain; Henry Dickerson McDaniel, first lieutenant; George S. Burson, second lieutenant; Eugenius C. Arnold, second lieutenant, junior grade; Josiah E. Nunnally, first sergeant; John T. Eckles, second sergeant; Richard E. Easley, third sergeant; William J. Richardson, fourth sergeant; Richard M. Preston, first corporal; Alexander H. Smith, second corporal; James N. Sheats, third corporal; Cicero P. Blasingame, fourth corporal; William C. Richardson, fifer, and Thomas G. Wood, drummer.

The colorful Captain George Thomas (Tige) Anderson, who had organized the company in Walton County, was promoted to colonel of the 11th Georgia Regiment, and in the wearying months to come Company H was to follow him, his hat waving in the air, the rebel yell reverberating from his throat, as he led his men into the terrifying heat of battle.

Captain Nunnally wrote more about army life in his letter to his sister: "and from this place [Confederate camp] I made my first march to Winchester, Va., a distance of twenty miles on one of the sultriest days of the year in about eight hours. We only rested about half the night because we had to prepare rations for that eventful march which will always be known in history as one of the severest of the war—the march to Piedmont, Va. (It will be remembered that we were not in the habit of marching). We marched a distance of thirty-four miles in less than twelve hours, in the meantime crossing the Blue Ridge. Words can but feebly portray the feelings of your brother at the end of that long but rapid march, here we were to take the cars to join Beauregard who was at that time fighting the enemy on the memorable plains of Manassas but owing to an accident on the road we failed to reach Manassas until the next day after the fight. Here I saw my first bloody battle field, here it was I heard the first groans of the wounded and dying; it was here I deeply felt the horrors of this terrible war, it was here I resolved that I should fight them as long as I could raise an arm."

The 11th Georgia was transported over the railway to Virginia and quartered in the new fair grounds at Richmond until July 15. Here the undisciplined troops were drilled in preparation for whatever the future might hold, a future which would include a role as Longstreet's "foot cavalry" and personal contact with the outstanding Confederate, General "Stonewall" Jackson.

Kittrell J. Warren of the 11th Georgia wrote of these days: "There has perhaps been no time since our enlistment during which the members of this regiment manifested such a general spirit of dissatisfaction; such restlessness under

PREFACE    xi

restraints; such murmurings at authority, and such complaints against the intolerable hardships of the war, as during the brief, bright period of our sojourn at the fair grounds. We drew abundant supplies of commissary stores, had delicacies in great quantities, sold for moderate prices within our guard lines; were convenient to as good water as the State affords; were securely protected from disagreeable weather by comfortable tents, provided with a profusion of blankets, equipped with numerous changes of raiment, and favored with cool shades under which to recline during our lazy hours; notwithstanding all of which we yet spent much time in dolorous repinings over the hardships of a soldier's life. We had enlisted to fight Yankees, not to sweep yards, clean away trash, stand guard in the rain, and, in short, embark in a general system of doing drudgery; and then to be compelled to ask a white man, no whiter than ourselves, for a pass in order to go beyond the guard lines, was such a discount upon the gentlemanly estimates we had formed of our gentlemanly selves. All these sad, insupportable disasters caused us to bend our anxious thoughts and longing hearts towards the quiet, pleasant homes we had so incautiously forsaken. Such is, no doubt, the experience of most soldiers in the service. The trying ordeals through which we have since passed will reveal themselves in their order.[2]

While this volume is built around the war letters of James Thomas Thompson, the youth who wrote his homefolk in his first message home, "All I want is a crack at a Yankey Boy," the story of the men in Company H is carried on after the death of James by three of his comrades: Kittrell J. Warren, the most prolific writer of the three, who a few months after Thompson's death returned home to become a state legislator; Captain Matthew Talbot Nunnally, about whom James wrote in such affectionate terms; and William T. Laseter, who later became a General of the United Confederate Veterans. Captain Nunnally met an untimely death in Devil's Den on July 2, 1863; the story is finished by William T.

Laseter, who lived through many battles before his story ended with the surrender of General Robert E. Lee at Appomattox.

### Acknowledgements

With only brief exceptions, the letters of James Thomas Thompson used herein were originally published in *The Virginia Magazine of History and Biography*, Vol. 70, No. 3, July 1962 (edited by Aurelia Austin). The original letters are owned by W. Carl Wells of Atlanta, Georgia, and they are reprinted with his kind permission.

The sixteen-page letter of Captain Matthew Talbot Nunnally is reproduced herein from a typescript furnished by Mrs. Martha S. Sullivan, niece of Captain Nunnally, who copied it from the original for use in this volume; I am indebted to her for her cooperation. My thanks also to the *Shreveport Journal* for its cooperation in furnishing a reproduction of the General William T. Laseter article.

My special appreciation to the three professors who so kindly gave of their time to read this manuscript and make helpful suggestions: Dr. Kenneth M. England, Dean of Students, Georgia State College; Dr. Bell I. Wiley, History Department, Emory University; and Dr. Willard Wight, History Department, Georgia Institute of Technology.

Aurelia Austin

*Atlanta, Georgia*

☆ | ☆

# "All I Want Is a Crack at a Yankey Boy"

"Thir Has bin another larg fight Hear at this place. . . . Thay taken great advantage of us by using secession flags; our loss not known," James Thomas Thompson wrote his family on July 23, 1861, from Bull Run, Virginia, two days after the battle of First Manassas. Although the battle of Bull Run is not considered by historians to have been a bloody battle, it is understandable that a young boy who had just left the peace and security of a Georgia plantation would find excitement in the "larg fight" that took place there.[1]

General Winfield Scott, who headed the Union armies, had felt that it would be wiser to train his green and undisciplined troops before beginning an invasion of the South. President Lincoln disagreed with Scott, being influenced by a demanding Congress and the loud clamorings of the Northern public whose slogan was "On to Richmond!"

Recently promoted Brigadier General Irvin McDowell was ordered to capture Richmond. He left Washington with approximately thirty-five thousand men and forty-nine artillery pieces. With the exception of a meager eight hundred, the troops were poorly trained militiamen and volunteers who knew nothing of fighting. On a hot July day McDowell set out along the Warrenton pike. He was accompanied by a strange assortment of newspaper reporters, sightseers, Congressmen, and even ladies in voluminous skirts. Some of the people crowded the road with their hacks and carriages, their picnic baskets stowed away carefully for future use.[2]

However, twenty-five miles southwest of Washington the atmosphere among the Confederate troops was not one of a gay holiday picnic. With twelve thousand less men and barely half as many guns, General Pierre G. T. Beauregard awaited the approaching blue-coated enemy.[3] The Confederate Army was stationed north of the village of Manassas, behind Bull Run. Guards were posted at the fords and roads leading to Richmond. Beauregard was to defend an important railroad junction from Alexandria, Virginia (opposite Washington), to Gordonsville and Richmond.

In the Shenandoah Valley, Confederate General Joseph E. Johnston was facing a Federal army of approximately twelve thousand men under the command of the veteran soldier, General Robert Patterson. With Johnston was the newly appointed Brigadier General, Thomas Jackson.[4] In order to go to the aid of fifty-three-year-old Beauregard it was necessary for Generals Johnston and Jackson to fool Yankee General Patterson, who had moved his army on the eastern side of the valley. Both Johnston and Jackson realized their enemy was headed towards Manassas in an effort to take Richmond, and that General Patterson was attempting to get between the Confederates and the gaps in the Blue Ridge in order to cut them off from General Beauregard.

By a clever bit of deception the two Confederate Generals turned the tables on the aged Patterson. Johnston ordered his forces to assemble near Winchester, as if he and Jackson intended attacking Patterson. Instead of making battle against that segment of the Union army, the Confederates marched quickly in the opposite direction, leaving only a portion of their troops to face Patterson. Kittrell J. Warren described the part played by the 11th Georgia in this deception:

"On the evening of the 15th we took passage in box cars (previously appropriated to the transportation of horses) up the Alexandria railroad, and having reached Manassas, journied thence to Strasburg, at which place we arrived late in the afternoon of the succeeding day, and found it a modest, neat little village of about 800 inhabitants, peeping out of the forest of surrounding mountains like a violet from the depths of a jungle. A short time after sunrise on the 17th, we began our first march, on foot, to Winchester, a distance of eighteen miles; and a wearying, disagreeable tramp it was. The sun shone warmly, and the cruel government had provided us with no umbrellas; clouds of floating dust almost stifled our breathing, and certainly succeeded in soiling our clean clothes and faces, and the hard macadamised road wore ugly blisters on our tender feet; but night found us at the point of destination, and requited our toils with deep and peaceful slumbers. The next day the Army of the Shenandoah, under General Joseph E. Johnston, evacuated Winchester and moved off to form a junction with and reinforce General Beauregard, preparatory to the great Manassas battle. Our blankets and knapsacks were deposited in wagons and we joined the brigade, then under command of Colonel F. S. Bartow, and marched on in the grand military procession. All night long the steady tramp was heard, and the moving multitude was seen crowding along the depths of the Shenandoah valley. Occasionally a loud, merry laugh would break upon the lonesome breeze, and anon the music of songs we had heard in happier days, came swelling through the midnight air, suggestive of home, and friends and bye-gone days, and the dim, dark, dreary-distance we had drifted from them, at which the mind recurred with sweet and soothing melancholy to the 'singing of the songs of Zion in a strange land.'

"About daylight we halted at Paris for an hour's rest. Notwithstanding our blankets, overcoats and most of our coats were in the wagons, and the morning, like mornings generally in this latitude, was cool, and although we had been without rations for near twenty-four hours, yet the necessity for rest and repose had become a ruling passion, and, in a few moments the roadside and sidewalks were literally lined and covered with a sleeping army. In the course of the day we reached Piedmont, and late in the afternoon drew rations and broke our long fast. Arrived at Piedmont, the army began to take passage for Manassas. Owing to a collision of the cars three regiments of our brigade, including the Eleventh, were left there until the 22d, and did not, therefore, participate in the battle."[5]

James Thompson complained, "Wee did not get here in time for the funn," but Dr. R. L. Dabney, in writing of how the men were moved from Winchester to Manassas, gave a plausible explanation for the delay of the 11th Georgia in reaching the battlefield:

"The president of the railroad company promised that the whole army should be transported on successive trains to Manassas Junction by the morning of Saturday, but by a collision which was, with great appearance of reason, attributed to treachery, the track was obstructed, and all the remaining troops detained, without any provision for their subsistence, for two precious days. Had they been provided with food, and ordered to continue their forced march, their zeal would have brought the whole of them to the field long before the commencement of the battle. General Jackson's whole command reached the Junction at dusk on Friday evening, and were marched, hungry, weary, and dusty, to the pine coppices near Mitchell's Ford, where they spent Saturday refreshing themselves for the coming conflict."[6]

In a letter to his parents, written at Piedmont, Virginia, on July 27, 1861, James Thompson has left us a picture of what happened to him during the period just prior to the battle.[7]

"Father & Mother. I am well at present. Hoping these few lines will finde you all Well. Wee ar all Well except Easley & Clay. Easley[8] Had a very Hard Chill yesterday. He is geting better. Clay Had 3 doctors with Him yesterday, but he is better. Wee left Richmond last monday Morning for Winchester. Wee march 20 miles to get thir. Wee Got thir on Wednesday night & left on thursday evening under force march of 65 miles to this place. Wee are now enrout for Masses junction wher Gen. Boragard Has bin fighting the

**BROTHERS OF JAMES THOMAS THOMPSON**
Top row, left to right: William and John; center: Wyatt; bottom row: Henry and Riley. A photograph of James is not available.

GENERAL THOMAS JONATHAN "STONEWALL" JACKSON
Courtesy of National Archives

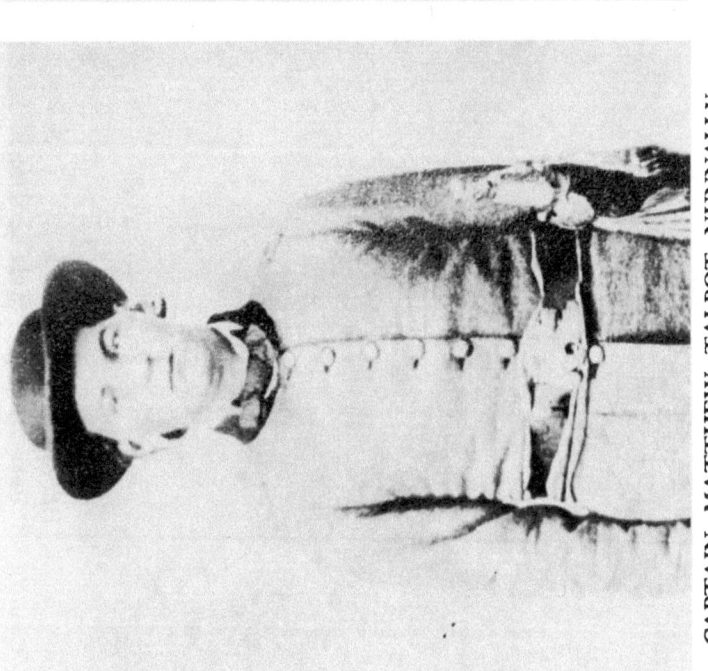

CAPTAIN MATTHEW TALBOT NUNNALLY
Courtesy of Mrs. George M. Napier, Monroe, Georgia

GEORGE THOMAS "TIGE" ANDERSON
Courtesy of Signal Corps, Brady Collection, National Archives

GENERAL JAMES LONGSTREET
Courtesy of Library of Congress

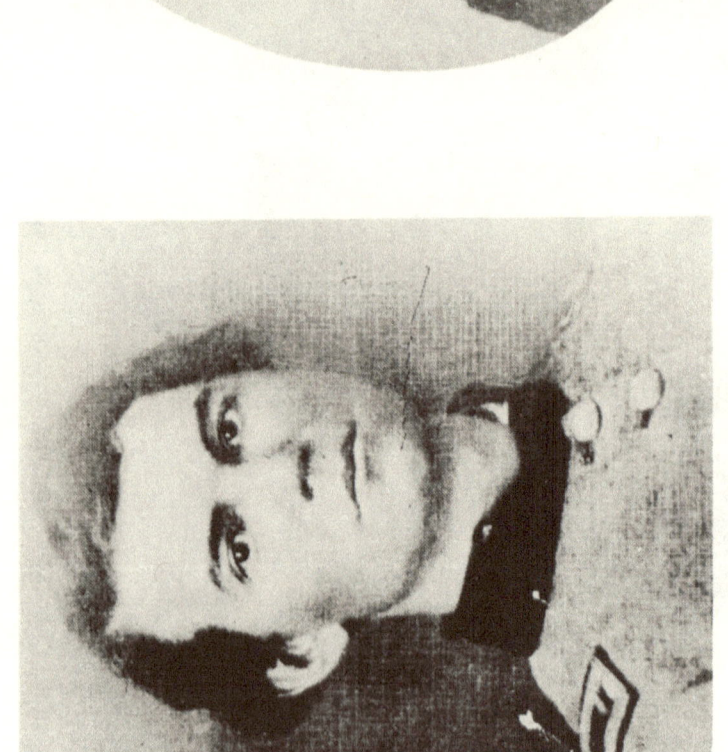

HENRY D. McDANIEL
Courtesy of Henry Tichenor, Monroe, Georgia

enemy. He beat them bac with the loss of 1500. Ours were only 70 killed and wounded. Wee are under Gen. Boragard. Wee start for Massas junction this evening. The boys all tuck the march very Hard. Thay blistered thir feete. Wee Had very bad lime stone water at Winchester which maid the boys verry sick, but as to my part i stood the trip very well. I wouldn't take $1000 for my trip Hear. All i want is a crack at a Yankey boy. I have seen all of the DeKalb Boys. They are all well except Captain Fowler & Seele Culwell. Thay are in the Hospittle at Winchester. Tell Wm. Singleton that John is well and fatend up the moast that i ever saw. Havel Cothron, Carroll Johnes, Powels Woodalls are as puney as ever &c.

"Agreeable to the beast [best] Railroad calcolations wee [are] 1160 miles[9] from Home. You need not write to mee untill i write again to you. . . . The boys all say i have faten up, and the oficers say i attend to my own buisiness about rite. I must bring my leter to a close. I will write more the next time. The captin says you can direct your letter to Richmond. Thay will be sent to us from thir, so write to mee soon.

Direct your letter to<br>
Private J. T. Thompson<br>
11 Ga. Regiment, Richmond, Va.<br>
In care of Col. C. T. Anderson"

The first fighting began on July 18 when Brigadier General James Longstreet, who was guarding Blackburn's Ford, routed a portion of McDowell's troops who had been sent to feel out the situation.

The main body of the Union army moved along the Warrenton Pike like a long gray snake, slowed down by excessive cooking and, as some historians think, "excessive caution." The slowness of the Union army gave the Confederates time to gather strength before the big battle. McDowell, who planned to attack the left flank of the enemy, left the Warrenton Pike and took a right to the Stone Bridge over Bull Run. Beauregard who had been a classmate of McDowell at West Point had planned the same type of attack. However, the Confederate left was saved by the alertness of the Signal Corps' E. P. Alexander, who got word to Major Nathan G. Evans that the Union Army was moving via Sudley Springs Ford. Evans was standing guard at the Stone Bridge on the Warrenton turnpike. Appraising the noise in front of him to be a feint, Major Evans had moved a large number of his forces to meet McDowell at Sudley Springs crossing.

General Johnston, who had also been informed of the flanking movement of the enemy, ordered Brigadier General Barnard E. Bee and Colonel Francis S. Bartow to go to the aid of their fellow Confederates. Wade Hampton's South Carolina aristocrats also joined in. However, the Union attack was fierce and difficult to withstand, and they drove the Confederates back in a state of confusion.

Confederates Bee and Bartow were killed, but before Bee died he called on his troops to rally behind the Virginia troops commanded by Brigadier General Thomas J. Jackson whose position was on a high point of the battlefield—Henry House Hill. It was Bee, on this occasion, who gave Jackson the sobriquet by which he was to become best known—"Stonewall" Jackson.[10]

Gunfire cracked fiercely back and forth over Henry House Hill, the home of an eighty-five-year-old widow, Mrs. Judith Henry. Confederates clad in blue uniforms captured two powerful Union batteries because their commander mistook his enemies for his fellow Federals. At 3:30 P.M., twenty-three hundred of Johnston's men, commanded by Kirby Smith, arrived from the Shenandoah Valley by rail and attacked McDowell's right flank, thus helping to decide the fate of the day in favor of the Confederate army.[11]

Kittrell Warren described how the 11th Georgia arrived at Manassas: "On the morning of the 22d, we took passage by railroad, and reached Manassas late in the forenoon, many of us compelled to take seats on top of the crowded cars and endure a cold and constant rain. After arriving, we waded through six miles of mud and water and camped in a low, ponded place on the northern margin of the battlefield, without the least possible protection from the falling weather. Our tents had been left at Winchester, and we afterwards held it quite a seal of veteranship that during the balance of the month we remained at that locality with no covering but blue skies and angry clouds."

The Federals retreated in a panic to Washington. Frightened men, among them many civilians, panicked on the Warrenton turnpike. Many of them even threw away their guns in order to travel faster. They discarded new canteens and knapsacks which the poorly equipped Confederates were glad to recover for themselves.

Between Sunday, July 21, and Tuesday, July 23, as James sat writing his brief note home, he probably listened eagerly to those who had participated in battle and gleaned some information, not exactly correct, about what had taken place. His comment to his family was:

"Wee did not get Hear in time for the funn. Wee will Have to burry the Yankeys today to keep them from stinking us to death. The Enemy loss about 2000 more or less, 1000 prseners. Wee got about 1500 stands of arms, 66 pecies of artilry."[12]

One can sense Thompson's disappointment that he did not reach Manassas in time for the "larg fight" to take a crack at a "Yankey Boy." But Thompson was not the only one who was disappointed. Although Stonewall Jackson had been the hero of the battle, he too was to come in for his share of disappointment following the battle. "If they will let me, I'll march my Brigade into Washington tonight," he was quoted as saying while he was having a wounded finger bandaged.[13]

On September 13, 1861, seven weeks after the Confederate victory at Bull Run, President Jefferson Davis met Major Generals Pierre G. T. Beauregard, Joseph E. Johnston, and Gustavus W. Smith at Centreville. Although the Generals advocated attacking Washington, Davis thought it unwise to withdraw from other Southern points troops necessary to wage so bold a battle.[14]

☆ II ☆

# "I Dreamp That God Was Sleaping with Mee"

"We camped near the field that summer," wrote Captain Nunnally. "Soon, however, my men commenced getting sick. I found that a camp could be made a hospital, for nearly everyone was sick. It was at this place I learned the agonizing pains of sickness. It became so frequent for one to die that I could lay in my tent and hear a poor mortal breathe his last without the slightest emotion. . . .

"At the latter part of our stay at this place I had my first sickness. I learned an important lesson here . . . how well it is to be blessed with health and how bad it is to be sick from home. I was prostrated four weeks with fever."[1]

The critical illness of his friend, Captain Nunnally, probably had its effect on young James, who was only twenty at the outset of the war. It is doubtful he had ever given much thought to eternity until he joined the army. Young James was enthusiastic about living, and his chief interests were good food, fancy clothes, the activities of his neighbors and friends, helping his father run a thousand-acre plantation,[2] girls to some degree, and music—but his greatest interest was in breeding fine horses. There had been no time to think about dying or whether or not he would continue to live beyond the grave.

Young James's tie to his Georgia home was strong, and only death was able to break it, although during his twentieth and twenty-first year he was destined to undergo a metamorphosis that not one of his family or friends could have predicted.

As a child James had been taught to respect his elders and this is evident in each of his letters to his parents; but at times he offered them some sound advice about the running of the plantation, and more especially in the field of religion which he felt better qualified than they to deal with. In signing his letters he used a business-like close, "Yours truly," but to young James it probably had a different meaning, "I am truly your obedient and loving son."

Obedience was the order of the day in the Thompson household. Without it life would have been bedlam, with three daughters (Mary Jane, Harriet, Elizabeth) and six sons (James, John, William, Wyatt, Henry, and Riley) running loose like wild animals.

The Thompson children learned responsibility early. There was a job for every child in the family as soon as he was able to understand how to execute a chore. There was the woodlot, where the cooking and fire wood must be cut, water to be drawn from the well, the garden to be weeded, the orchards to be tended, vegetables and fruits to be gathered, candles to be molded, soap to be made, and spinning, weaving and knitting to occupy long winter days. These chores were divided among the younger boys and the three girls, but care of the horses was the detail assigned to James, and it became his special delight. Tending horses gives one time to become aware of the inner man and to make plans for the future.

Thomas Thompson believed in work because it had made him the wealthiest man in at least one county. His plantation home, a mushroom sort of frame house, had grown with his family's needs. He also owned other property, some of it located in thriving Atlanta.[3]

While Thomas Thompson's beautiful wife, Lucinda Hardman Thompson, was a real Southern aristocrat—the daughter of John Hardman and Mary Cochran of Lexington, Georgia, and the great-granddaughter of Revolutionary War soldier,

John, and his wife, Elizabeth, of Halifax County, Virginia—Thomas Thompson had fought his way up the hard way. As a boy Thomas was poor. He earned his first money to buy land by digging ditches, and he prided himself on being not only a hard worker, but a sober man.

Thomas taught his six sons to work hard and to be sober and morally sound, but there was an absence of religious fervor in the Thompson home before the war. God was someone to be feared when thought about at all. He was the Giver of life and the Reaper in death. He was the Judge of the world and one avoided Him whenever possible. Thomas Thompson had been so busily engaged in providing for a family of eleven that he had not spent any time worrying about God and what might happen to him after death, nor had he spent any time serving God. He had lived for himself and his family only.[4]

Young James joined the Confederate Army before he realized that religion was of any importance. Then the inner man began to show changes.

While there were green country boys in the Confederate Army who learned to gamble, to curse, and to drink liquor, and in some instances to indulge in a free and easy sex life with the prostitutes who followed the army, there were some like James Thompson who abstained from these practices.[5] In October of 1861 James commented to his father, "My Captain choosed me from among the whole co. to do their cooking, because i Dident play cards, swair, and so on."

He was also careful with his money. On July 27, 1861, James wrote home, "Some of the boys are sending home for money. I hav spent 50 cts since I left Atlanta, 30 of that for postage." He was also aware of his responsibilities to his family, for on January 6, 1862, he wrote, "I sent you $85 by R. S. Easly. I intend to send youe more as soon as Wee Draw again."

Apparently sometime during the early part of the first summer of the war, young Thompson was converted. There is no mention in any of the James Thompson letters that an inner search took place such as many of his generation experienced before conversion: the state of alarm brought about by the "hell fire" preaching of evangelists; witnessing the happiness of friends and relatives who had surrendered and envying them their peace of mind; a period of increasing unrest and inner conflict and a conviction of sin that plunged one into the dark pit of despair; and then the final moment of joy and flood of comfort when one surrendered his life to God and felt forgiven of his old sins.

It is readily apparent that young James must have attended religious services held by the few who ministered to the spiritual needs of Stonewall Jackson's men, and soldiers serving under other officers of comparable rank. Apparently these older men made an ineradicable impression on James and helped him find a rare companionship with God—a peace and companionship which caused him to write his mother and sisters on August 12, 1861 from Camp Bartow[6] in Prince William County, Virginia, and tell them in simple, direct words about his conversion:

"It is said that the soalgers life is an unhappy one, but with me it is a happy one, for i hav maid peac with my God. I hav praid to him for forgivness. I Dreamp that God was sleaping with mee. Thir is not a day but what I offer up a prair."

Then he does what every reborn child of God longs to do—the thing the shepherds did when they had found and worshipped the Christ Child in His Manger—he wanted others to share in his enriching experience. In the same letter to his mother and sisters in which he told of his own conversion, he included a plea to his loved ones to search until they too had found this new peace and eternal happiness:

"Dear mother and sisters, Give up your harts to God, for he is merciful to all whoo seaks him. Go and join the Church and try to serv him, for now is the time for you know not when you will be called to a world unknown to thee. Oh parents, call up the children around the chearful fireside and read a portion of the scriptur to them, and be shure to Hould

Family prair. . . . Dont say that you will do better after while. Dont think that you will be slited in Company, for you will not be in the sight of God. Join Any Church that you pleas. . . . Go amediatly. Don't wait till tomorrow [to do] what you should do today. Evry Night Get the Bible, Call Evry one around you and offer up a prair to your Dear Saivior for Great will be your reward. Mother and sisters . . . as an Elder Son and Elder Brother, it is my only wish and Harts Desire that you may Giv up your whole harts to God. If i never meet you in Georgia i hope to in the pairradise of God. I will Come to a close by promising to write to you again. Please write to mee for i wish to hear from you.

James T. Thompson"[7]

Between August 12 when young Thompson wrote his family, "It is said the soalgers life is an unhappy one, but with me it is a happy one" and October 30, 1861, the date of his next letter, Stonewall Jackson was not as happy as Thompson. The General was lonely for his Anna and somewhat discouraged about the state of affairs.

The weather was oppressively hot, and the water was bad. Many of the men were sick, and camp life was monotonous with drilling and artillery practice every day for those who had remained well enough to be up and about.

Warren reported, "On the 2d of August the regiment moved to and established what was subsequently designated 'Camp Bartow,' to the right of the Alexandria railroad, three miles above Manassas. Here we remained for more than a month, rendered unfit for duty by the prevalence of measles. Unfavorable weather, uncomfortable hospital tents, no disinfectants, and almost no physic, were circumstances which caused the disease to rage with more than ordinary virulence. Day after day did the indefatigable Means (now considered one of the best surgeons in the service) move among the tents, administering words of cheer and the best relief in his power to the languishing and afflicted; while the wise, experienced, sagacious and kind-hearted Colley stood ever at the door of his hospital, spectacles riding his nose, and bearing in front a stomach, whose huge, ponderous and corpulent protrusion denoted that it had been the cemetery of many generations of pork and collards, compelled from sheer necessity (Sangrado-like) to prescribe on the paper he held in his hand "C.M." pills and a solution of diluted bread, to make measles break out, and a like dose of diluted bread and 'C.M.' pills to scatter the eruption."[8]

Company H remained at Camp Bartow until September 11 when it was ordered northward ten miles. Here the men pitched their tents near Pine Branch. About 10:00 P.M. that evening they marched to a new campsite (a distance of four miles) to a place near Fairfax Courthouse.[9] On September 25, Company H was detailed for picket duty at Winder's Hill and marched to Falls Church, where it remained until the morning of the 28th. The men covered the retrograde movement of Confederate troops to Mills Road and were relieved there and returned to camp on October 1st.[10]

Captain Nunnally recorded, "Little occured at this camp of importance except that we made some very hard marches and came in close proximity to the Abolitionist and performed our first picket duty. . . . During this march it rained very hard, the roads became very muddy and we had to march all night without a moment to close our eyes. I thought on this march that I could ring the necks from every Yankee in existence if only I had a chance."[11]

Warren relates a humorous incident that took place during the rainstorm alluded to by Captain Nunnally: "As we stood dripping over a fire after the completion of our march a soldier said, 'I'll tell you mister that was a rale scrougin rain. The cloud hit kum bulgin over us, and the warter hit commenst a drapen outen them ar little gimblet holes what's bord through the bottom to let the rain out, when all of a suddent, the cloud hit josselled up agin somethin and upsot, and split hitself right all in among us, and hoop! how the thunder and lightnin did have to jump to get outen the cloud afore it hit the yeath.' "[12]

Warren wrote further, "The enemy not having advanced

to meet us as was expected, we returned the next morning, and four days afterwards moved up and camped on the Braddock road one and a half miles from Fairfax Courthouse."[13]

"From this point," continued Warren, "we went to Falls church, a distance of twelve miles, to discharge our first picket duty during the 25th. On our arrival we were met by the exciting intelligence that the foe had marshaled his cohorts and was advancing in force. We tore down fences and other coverts, removed obstructions from the front, aligned ourselves in a tenable position, and awaited the anticipated advance. But with the exception of a foraging party, which was repelled and dispersed by two pieces of the Washington artillery, supported by the 9th Georgia, no enemy appeared on that occasion. On the night of the 27th, a flank movement being apprehended, our pickets were drawn in. At the time the orders came, six companies of the regiment under command of Capt. Stokes, were occupying Nutt's hill, three miles above the church. Their clothes were wet from the effects of a rain that afternoon, the weather had cleared off cold and windy, and their proximity to the Yankee lines being such (about three hundred yards) as to render it imperatively necessary to observe the utmost stillness, the order to fall back was of course agreeable, as it put in motion the benumbed and shivering limbs of the soldiers. Captains Stokes and Luffman having completed the discharge of their duties, had just before taken temporary quarters in a hut near the line, and there they remained, overlooked by the courier and wholly unconscious of the exodus of their commands, cracking jokes and spinning yarns, until long after the hill had been abandoned to the enemy. But, *per gratia*, the darkness of the night, the sluggishness of the foe, and the genial influence of their own lucky stars, they uncaptured and rejoined their companies before the regiment left Falls church. After falling back three and one-half miles, we halted near daybreak, at the junction of the Alexandria and Fairfax roads. During the day the enemy occupied the church, and late in the afternoon rumors of an advance were confidently circulated. But the enemy came not, and having lain on arms for three days awaiting their arrival, our relief came and we repaired to camps. The seasons of quietude which occur at occasional intervals of our history, as they are occupied in drilling, standing guard, cooking, washing, and going through the usual monotony of camp life, possess, of course, no features which are noteworthy, and must, therefore, be treated with silence.

"The cold season was now approaching, and on the 15th of October the process of concentration, preparatory to the coming winter, was begun. Signal rockets having gone up long ere the break of day, the roll of drums from field and forest, hill and hamlet, for miles around, summoned the drowsy army from their peaceful slumbers, and indicated that important designs were marked out on the military tressel board. Our regiment was formed, remained in position until after daylight, and then broke ranks, ate breakfast and once more went on picket. [In the rear of Indian's House.] The position assigned us in this instance was six miles above Fairfax and about two to the left of the Anandale road. The army was now retreating to, and massing around Centreville, and a corresponding change in the outpost became therefore necessary. Accordingly the next morning were ordered in, and having passed through Fairfax, we camped for the night at Germantown, an antiquated village, situated one mile to the west of Fairfax.

"The subsequent day was devoted to the removal of valuables from the latter place, and our regiment was detained to protect the transportation. In the afternoon General Wadsworth, the recently defeated candidate for Governor of New York, with a force of infantry and cavalry, advanced within half a mile of the Court-house. Couriers hurried to and fro, the long roll was beaten, and expectation stood tiptoe for a raid, in which the redoubtable General would unquestionably have been caged, but he cautiously retired without making any additional demonstration.

"About dark we took up the line of march down Little River turnpike, again attended by that disagreeable companion, a continuous and pouring rain. At some points the road was slippery, at some boggy, and at others the yielding soil seemed beaten into a sort of musilaginous batter."

Captain Nunnally corroborated the story about the sticky mud in the following comment: "In the meantime our camps were moved from Fairfax C.H. to Centerville. We remained out on picket some two or three days more and we went to Centerville finally, our camp pitched on the muddiest spot in the county."

Somewhere—perhaps on picket duty—James Thompson caught a cold that was so severe he was sent to the No. 2 Georgia Hospital, located on Twentieth Street in Richmond, Virginia. The reader of his letters is left wondering whether by that time he still felt his original high enthusiasm for a "soalgers life." It is possible Thompson had already been assigned to the cooking detail.

In October James Thompson was an assistant nurse, passing out medicine, despite his cold germs, to his fellow soldiers who were less fortunate than he.

"Richmond, Virginia
October the 30th, 1861

"Thomas Thompson,
Stone Mountain, Geor.

"I Seat myself to inform you that i am Geting along very well. Hoping thes few lines will find you all Well. I fixed up to go to camps but Was not clear of cold and the Doctors toald mee I Had beter stay untill . . . my lungs got sound. Our Doctors ar all Georgians. Wee Hav Dr. Williams from Walton county to wait on us. Thir is part of 3 companies of Walton boys on this flore in cear [care of] Dr. Williams. I hav not taken any medicin sinc I hav bin hear only for my cough. Thir has [been] another battle. It was at Leesburg, Va. near the Potomac. General [N. G.] Evans commands our forces. Thir loss is about 1500, our loss not very Great.

They brought in about 680 prisners to this place. I saw them When they landed to the Depo. Thir was 22 officers among them. Some of them Giv right up, never tried to Defend themselves at all. Thay sed thay about to starve. 300 Wer Drowned in the Potomac, some ar Deserting an coming over among us. Thay ar taken garded. Thay ar not called prsners, but Deserters. I think Thay ar treated beter than prsners. Thir is Hardly a Day but what thir is more or less prsners coming in from some whir. The papers say that wee are whiping the Federals by liing abou Doin nothing. Wee Got sevrel pieces of artilry beside several stands of arms.

"Some of the Georgia Regiments Hav bin orderd to North and South Carrolina. Benjamin Easley is hear. His son is sick at the first Georgia Hospul. His son is Liutenent of a Co. He heard that i Was at the 2 Hospial. He come to see mee, but i Was Gon out. I think he has Gon up towards Manassas to see Daniel and Luther. Thay ar at the Culpepper Hospital sick. I [am] still assistan nurs. I Giv out medicine. I go to the table With the Doctors, [and] . . . get anything that i want to eat, Which the rest of the boys ar Deprived of. Som of the boys says thay bliev that i could Get into office any whire. I Did not volunteer my servis Atall. My Captain choosed mee from among the Whole co. to do thir cooking, because i Dident play cards, swair, and so on. When i left camps thay toald mee to stay untill i Got sound if it was 3 months [and that] i should Hav my place when i come back. . . . My Regment is at Centersville, 7 miles to the left of Manassas. All of our troops hav left Fairfax and come back this Way about 18 miles . . . the lincon [Lincoln] boys Wants rom for a fair fight between us and the Potomac. Thay Got pleanty of room. . . . I will bring my letter to a close. . . . Write just as soon as u reciv this. Direct your letter to
                    James T. Thompson
                    Richmond, Va.
                    2 Georgia Hospital, Box 961"[14]

The No. 2 Georgia hospital in which Thompson spent two months or more before Christmas was formerly a tobacco warehouse. The hospital was financed by funds contributed by the Georgia Hospital and Relief Association, with headquarters in Augusta, Georgia. The Association was a voluntary organization until December 1861, when the state made appropriations of $1,500,00 in the next four years for the upkeep of four hospitals in Virginia and twelve hospitals in Georgia, in addition to a number of "wayside homes."

The chaplain who was in charge of religious work at the several Georgia hospitals in Richmond wrote the following to the *Southern Christian Advocate*:

"We are using as hospitals, three tobacco factories . . . affording very good accommodations for hospital purposes. Coverlets and quilts are from Georgia homes. I have visited many hospitals in Richmond, but have found none so well arranged, and so well managed as the Georgia Hospitals. . . . The hospitals are visited by our Representatives in Congress, especially Vice-Pres. Stephens who is a constant visitor."

Other prominent visitors to these Georgia hospitals were the wives of General Robert Toombs and Captain Harris of Marietta.

Two weeks after his first letter was written from the No. 2 Georgia Hospital, Thompson wrote his parents a second letter. There is no mention of his having received a letter from home in the meantime, but perhaps he wished to reassure his mother in case she might be worried about him, as he did in later letters.

"Richmond, Virginia
Thursday, November the 14th

"I seat myself to inform you that . . . i expect to stay hear until Christmas. The Doctors wants mee to stay a Whil longer and i think i had better. . . . If i stay hear i will still Draw my 11 dollars per month. I Get just anything i want to eat as i am an assistant nurs. The Doctors has anything you could call for, and i eat with them corn bread, buiscuit, bacon, Cabag, beef, poark, muton, Fish, Oisters, chickens, butter milk, and such like. My Cough is better but i have some cold yet. . . . You must write to mee if Flowers Co. has left

# I DREAMP THAT GOD WAS SLEAPING WITH MEE

Geor. yet. . . . Several of my company come hear with mee, but hav Got Discharges and Gon home, 6 of them this week. Dr. [William S.] Barrett & Dr. McBeen [David S. McBean] say i had beter get a discharge and Go back to Georgia and spend the Winter anyhow, but i Dont Want to come Home by no means at all. The Way times ar now the Yankies ar advancing on us at Sentersville Which is on one side of the Manassas Battle Ground. Thay want to try us again on Manassas plains. I hav my information from the telegrath Dispach this morning. I Wish i was thir to stand by my noble young Captains side and fight them untill we conkered them.

"You Wanted to know in what book to find Numans beef act. . . . You will find one book that you and McCurdy bought in Athens when McCurdy cared [carried] Messenger[15] over in Jackson. . . .

       Yours Truly,
       James T. Thompson[16]
2nd Geor. Hospital, 20th St.
Box 961, Richmond, Va."

☆ III ☆

# "I Enjoy Camp Life Better Than Anybody Els I Recon"

There were better educated[1] and better trained men in army tactics than James Thomas Thompson, but none who volunteered his services to the Southern cause could boast of greater enthusiasm for the hard life a Confederate soldier must lead. His enthusiasm was not of the "here today and gone tomorrow" variety, but it maintained the same level throughout the entire period he was a participant in the war. In James's letters there was a marked absence of the usual "beefing" engaged in by the average soldier of any war, and his love and admiration for his officers was without stint.

"Camp Centersville, Virginia
December the 11th, 1861
"Father, I Received your letter on the 8th dated Nov. the 30th. It come threw in 8 days. . . . I enjoy camp life better than any Body els i recon, without it is Tom Anderson. Nothing els suites Him better than a soalgers life. I Hav nothing of importance to write. We hav very fine wether now for the last 8 or 9 days. It seems all moast like summer. . . . Wee hav just come in of ov picket gard. Wee hav to Go out on picket Evry 2 Weaks. I am with the officers yet, and when Wee wer out on picket i carry out qite flower [flour] enough to do us untill the last meel. When wee wer eating i dident hav bread enough to do us all. Captin Nunnally Went off and got bread and devided it with me. . . .

What he has, apples, cakes or anything, he devids with me. He is as fine a man as ever lived. My first and second liutenants ar the same way, but Arnold the 3rd lutenant . . . had bin off sick all the time before i went . . . to the Hospital, and When i come Back . . . becaus everything Was not to his notion he Would Grumble. I thought he Was not saddisfied with me. I went to Captin Nunnally and toald Him i thought Arnold Was disaddisfied and i had rather quit unless all was agreeable. He said i should stay With them. He said he was well pleased with mee, all so the 2 first Luitenants. Arnold is a brother to the lawyer that foold Michum out of the $50. They had 2 or 3 cooking for them While i was at Richmond and he was not sadisfid With none of them. I try to pleas all of them, but he wants his vituals cooked difrent from the rest. I umor him the best i can and i expect to stay with Captin Nunnally as long as Wee boath stay in sirvis. 2 of the Tiger rifelsmen from New Orleans Wer shot yesterday for carying bayonets on a Liutenant. . . ."[2]

Apparently the summer-like weather did not last long, as Captain Nunnally wrote his sister: "Soon after this it began to be quite cool and the weather became very disagreeable. For it rained every other day and snowed in the intervals. So the boys had to seek some method by which they would be a little more comfortable. They first introduced what is called underground chimneys, but this plan failed and they fell upon the plan of the oldfashioned stick and dirt chimney. This made us as comfortable as one could ask. You cannot imagine how pleasant it will make a tent to have one of these chimneys in it. A tight room with a splendid fire-place can be but little better. We lived luxuriously in this pleasant camp life until the twenty-fifth of December. Then we commenced erecting large spacious & huge edifices in the shape of ten by twelve log huts. I moved into mine the eighth of January eighteen hundred sixty-two. I will not attempt to give you a description of its exterior appearance nor of its interior adornments for it certainly never was intended for the pen to place upon paper nor the mind of man to express it in words. We passed our leisure moments in these huts quite pleasantly; we amused ourselves at the different card games, draft, etc., etc., and frequently many pleasant hours were whiled away with our fine Killi-Kin Nick (smoking tobacco) and Meerchaums. Occasionally having it mixed with Eggnog. We feasted upon all the luxuries of the Old Dominion, our table was supplied most bountifully with fat beef served in various styles, nice bread, potatoes, ham, eggs, coffee, syrup, etc."[3]

Warren recalled that "The regiment continued to discharge picket duty at the position here referred to during occasional intervals of the ensuing winter. As the neighborhood was not infested, not even threatened with Yankees, afforded quantities of cheap provisions, fire-wood in abundance, and moreover some charming and musical specimens of the sweeter sex, it is not to be wondered at that their recurrence grew in favor with the soldiers and became quite a holiday pastime."[4]

Captain Nunnally reminisced, "Many times do I recur to our old winter quarters as the spot where my most happy moments of my soldiering life were spent. But lo! our stay at this place was of but short duration."[5]

Apparently picket duty and five snows, not to mention the rain, did not dampen Thompson's enthusiasm for army life, for he continued to write his father enthusiastic reports.

"Camp Centersville, Virginia
January the 6, 1862

"Father, I Reciv 2 letters from Home, I receiv one from the Girls With the fine come [comb] in it. I Was glad to get the come, for thay cant be Had hear. I Recived one from you & Marian Dated December 21st. I was glad to hear from you Boath. I Was sorry to hear of so many fiers. I believ Georgia is full of Black republicans. We Hav bin called to healp the suffers of Charlston Whoo was ruined by fier. I put $1. . . . Johny Sprewel sent my boots to mee by Samuel Fields Whoo brought shooes for the Yellow Dogs. I paid for the boots myself. Thay cost me $8. Thay ar

Doubble sole, Water proof. I could hav got $15 for them before i ever saw them. If you pleas, Write to John that i have got the Boots & paid Fields 8 Dollars for them. Thay just fit mee & i am Well pleased With them. . . . Giv my best respects and wishes to Aunt Matilda & Elizor Gober for the socks. Tell them i am Grafully thankful for them. . . . You never hav Wroat to mee how much corn & Wheat you maid. I begrug the mule that you let Newman [Pounds] Have for i thought it was the best animal of the kind i Ever saw. I Want you to use my mair When ever you want to, & if she brings a coalt next spring & Does well i Want you to put Hear [her] to the beast horse you can find, for the people ar not raising any now and horses Will be Worth some thing if peace is ever maid. Write to mee how the mair is geting along & What has become of Waid, and if Kelly is still living on your land yet, & has he ever paid youe any rent. . . . I must come to a close as i Want to Write a few lines to Mother and the Girls.

Yours Truly,<br>James T. Thompson

P. S. Father, Wee have moved into Winter quarters. The name of our camp is Camp Sam Jones."[6]

"Camp Sam Jones<br>2nt Brigaid, 11th Division<br>Army of the Potomac, Va.<br>February the 8th, 1862

"Father, I Hav nothing of importanc to write you. Wee hav rain and snow a pleanty. Wee hav had 5 snows. I got in of ov picket las Monday night. Thir come 2 snows on us while wee were out thir. Our first Liutenant [Henry D. McDaniel][7] and ordily Sargent Has gone Home to get recruits for our company. Wee want 20 recruits if thir is any Body in our settlement that Wants to get into one of the largest companys that Georgia Has ever raised. . . . Tell them to come to the Walton infantry. Thay started Home yesterday. . . . I want you to bring my things down to Monroe,

Ga. Lietenant Henry D. McDaniel said he would bring them for mee. Put them into as small a box as you can, so it will be as little trouble as possible to Handle. Put in 2 pair Drawers, Fateag shirt, 2 or 3 pair socks, as it may be the last chance to Get anything from Home. Put in 2 pair Home maid suspenders and my Feather Hat, if the boys has not wore it out. Send mee some redd peper, little saig, if you Hav it, all so a little allum. Tell mother to send my cloaths that i left in my trunk. Send mee 1 or 2 pair pants. I think i Had 1 or 2 pair that i had maid last Spring. . . .

I Hav Gon back to the companie for a While. The sutlers has Gon Home. When thay come back the officers Wants mee again . . . .

Yours truly<br>J. T. Thompson[8]

[P. S.] Pleas put Masons & Skiners Horse fairier in with the rest of the things."[9]

One can picture young James Thompson sitting around a campfire in the colorful autumn woods of Virginia, or perhaps as a patient in one of the Georgia hospitals, talking enthusiastically about horses. Perhaps he was saying, "When the first shots of the war were fired at Fort Sumter I was over in Walton County with Messenger, my father's fine stallion."

His letters to his father written during this period reveal that he was in Walnut Grove (near Monroe, Georgia) on April 12, 1861. After paying for a night's lodging at Mr. Taners', and some other expenses, he had $15 to send to his father towards the expenses of running Thomas Thompson's plantation.

In this letter he wrote, "I Hav sent for the American Stock Journal. I am making up a club for it. You will Get a spesamen coppy of it befor long. I Dont Want you to lend out that Morgan Horse book to no one for I am detirmin to learn all about the hors that i can. Excuse my bad Hand Write Father. Male [Mail] is waiting."[10]

In James Thompson's letters to his father in the spring of 1860, written from Walnut Grove and Monroe, large sums of money were enclosed as stud fees from Messenger. During this period Mr. Hight, a delegate to the Milledgeville convention, helped young Thompson arrange bookings for Messenger. Thompson delighted in his responsibilities and commented, "Some says that i am as good a groom as thay ever saw. I Dont know about that. I keep plenty of leevs & straw in his stables. He eats Harty. I keep a Popler pool [pole] in each one of his stables which he eats the bark of."[11]

Thompson's knowledge of horses apparently impressed his officers, some of whom had probably known him while he was in Walton County with Messenger, and he was asked to become a "horsler," or perhaps they had seen him reading "Mason and Skinner's Horse fairier" which he had requested his father to send to him with his clothes.

"Camp Sam Jones, Virginia
February the 17th, 1862

"Yours Dated January 31 came to Hand on the 9th Inst. I Was Glad to hear from all. Looks like that you all mite Write more oftiner than you do. I think i dont reciv more than from one to 2 a month. I learn that thir Will soon be a draft in Georgia and i dont cear How soon evry man Will Have to come. . . . The Yankies Whiped us out at Ronoak, North Carrolina, but Wee hav Whiped them out at Fort Donelson, Tennessee. Tom Anderson Has not bin promoted yet, but is acting Brigadier Genral. Yet if Wee get our 20 recruits Wee will hav the largest company in the brigaid. . . . Wee Get plenty to eat and the new rail rodd is about finished from Manassas to Sentersville. I think Wee will Get to favor our Horses some now as our hauling will be done by the cars.

"I went out on picket last week. I saw 8 Horses dead and another lying all most life less on the Ground. I saw this many just passing the rodd from camps to the picket line. If people dont Go to raising Wee Will bee obliged to suffer.[12] You said if you did not Get King to keep Messenger that you was

Going to put Bob[13] out With him. I dont [think] that Will do Well, but you no best. Negroes ar Hiring so cheap i think you had better Hier a Negro man and put him to clearing and ditching, and hav the Willow pack [patch] and colt paster cleaned up, all so the peace above the spring, and the peac by the old mulbery tree. If you will Hier one and put him at it i will help you to pay his hier, as it is the opinion of all that the War is comeing to a close. . . . Easly is very Bad off. Daniel is Geting beter. . . .

"The assistant quarter master Has bin after mee today. He wants mee for a Horsler. Wee hav taken our old tents and streached them on poals and stakes and maid a stable nearly 100 feet long, maid on the plan of a regular livery stable, with a row of horses on each side. The assistant quarter master is a member of our companie, and ses that he thinks that i noe something about horses, and ses that i will attend to mi buisiness. I dont noe whirter I shal Go to the stable or not. . . ."[14]

In spite of Thompson's great love for horses, there is no mention in his further letters that he accepted the Assistant Quartermaster's offer to become a "horsler." Perhaps this was due to moving orders being issued on March 8, as was reported by Warren.

"On the 8th day of March moving orders were issued, accompanied by the announcement that Gen. McClellan was pressing hard upon our rear and flanks with overpowering numbers. Hitherto, amid all the vicissitudes the regiment had undergone, we managed to preserve a sufficiency of clothing, blankets and tents. Now transportation was furnished to officers alone, and that under circumstances which denoted that the recovery of the articles transported would be indefinitely postponed, and attended perhaps with very considerable risks and disadvantages. Privates were compelled to abandon everything they could not carry. We were gradually becoming more deeply involved in the severe trials and rough usages of war." Warren states that the weather and roads were indescribable to his Georgia friends and goes on to say, "Our march lay through Gainsville and Warrenton, by Warrenton Springs, and to Culpeper, which place we reached on the 11th, and rested for three days. From Culpeper we proceeded to Orange, where we arrived and pitched our tents near Montpelier, the former residence of President Madison, on the 17th, after having crossed the Rapidan on bridges we had constructed of wagons."[15]

Captain Nunnally also wrote to his sister about the move. "On the morning of the eighth of March at an early hour we were informed by the tap of the drum that we were to bid adieu to winter quarters. We left on that long to be remembered morning we knew not for where, but soon found out that we were travelling in the direction of Orange C. H. on the Rapid Ann [sic] River a distance of sixty miles. . . . The weather was delightful for this season of the year. Slightly cool, making a blanket or a couple of them quite comfortable at night. We were something over a week in reaching our journey's end. We remained at Orange about a month, nothing transpiring but the usual monotony of camp life."

Some surprises were in store for Nunnally and Thompson and all the other Confederates, but James Thompson's enthusiasm for army life had not then been thoroughly wet by wading the Potomac four times in three different places. In his letter which follows, young James was trying to reassure his Mother and sisters.

> "Centerville, Virginia
> Corng. Court House
> March the 26, 1862

"Dear Mother and sisters, I seat myself to answer your letter Which i recived this evning. . . . Mother, you said you never lay down without thinking of mee. Dont Griev or be troubled about me, and as to lying on a soft feather bead [bed] i lie just as comfortable as i want to. I can take 2 blankets and lie down in a pile of rocks, or in the mud on frozen Ground, or anywhir without anything to shelter with. My Cotrig Box makes a soft pillow, the Mother Earth makes a easy bed, the heavens makes a good shelter, the Lord is a

Good genral. You must think when you lie down that our Saiviour Had nowhir to lay His head. Trust in God and alls Well . . . The Great Washington went hungry and raged, lay on the coald, frozen ground without blankets, then why not mee be lik Washington. I Glory in the honor and pride of a solgers life. Nothing suits me better. I hav Good officers. I love them, thay love mee, and all ways will. My colonel gives mee praise. Wee have 125 men in our companie. Wee love each other like a band of brothers, and i try to act so as to Gain love and confidence of all. . . . Whirever you see a larg companie you see Good officers. When you see a small companie you see mean officers.

"Liutenant McDaniel brought my cloathes on to Richmond. He left his one [own] clothes and mine thir. Thay Will be on in a few days. You said you was greaving about the Ham and cakes. McDaniel brought the ham and cakes threw. The cakes and ham is very nice. We draw hams, but not as fine as the one you sent me. . . .

J. T. Thompson"[16]

It was fortunate that McDaniel left his and Thompson's clothes in Richmond, as Thompson described to his father in a letter also written on March 26 the trouble they experienced moving the army and some of the disasters that occurred.

"Camp near Orange Court House
Corng. County, Va.
March the 26th, 1862

"I seat myself to inform you i am Well. . . . Hoping thes few lines may find you all enjoying the same. I hav nothing mutch to write, only wee have retreated back about 60 to 70 miles and Distroyed Briges and rail roads as wee retreated, so as if the enemy persoued us thay would be Detained. They wer advancing rapidly on us at Centersville. I learn yesterday that the Merilanders Wer about to take Washington City and the Yankies had to go back to keep them down. I learn the Yankies or all Gon back on thir . . . side of the Potomac.

Wee had to burn up nearly all of our cloathes, and bagag. Wee were on the road 11 days. The train of wagons were put in frunt of the army for protection. The train of wagons was about 10 miles long, and so Heavey loaded that thay couldent Get along fast through the Deep, stiff mud, for it was raining moast of the time. Wee lay over 4 days at Culpeper Court House, so as the Wagons might Get a long Ways ahead of us. I tell you it is trouble to moov such a large army. You could see men Giv out and lie down on the coald, wet ground. The Generals Had Gards put behind the army to take up every man that fell out of ranks and evry man that was able to march thay maid them Go on. Them that Wer not able was put on the cars and sent to Richmond. I saw sevral horses lying in the middle of the road completly giv out. Thir was more blankets throan away on the march than horse teem could pull, and cloaths of the very best kinde. Evry company sufferd very mutch from fatedg, except our companie. Wee hadnt Got fair [far] from our old camps befor Captin Nunnally bought a Wagon and splendid teem and had our knapsacks hawled. . . . Wee had the best Captin in sirvis. He is kind to us and favours us all he can. You wanted mee to go with Hoile or Fowler, but i am in the best companie yet. I would not quit my larg and splendid companie.

J. T. Thompson"[17]

Captain Nunnally reminisced to his sister that "On the tenth of April we left this place on the cars for Richmond, Va., where we remained two days and we embarked on board a schooner on the James River for Yorktown, Va. The enemy at this time was threatening this point in large forces. We arrived in due season to retard the progress of the foul invader."[18]

On April 12, 1862, Union General George B. McClellan landed an army of 105,000 men at Fort Monroe, in an effort to capture Richmond.[19]

The day that Yankee General McClellan landed his large force at Fort Monroe, James Thompson was at Camp Winder writing about the march to Fredericksburg.

"Camp Winder
Richmond, Va.
Apr. the 12, 1862

"Father, I seat myself this morning to Drop you a few lines to let you know that i am well and Harty.... Monday & Tuesday Wee had snow and sleet a pleanty. Wee were out in it all. Wee left Orng. Court House on Sonday evning to the fight at Fredericksburg. Wee marched all night threw the rain and marched moust all day Monday. Got nearly to Fredericksburg. Wee learn the enemy had fell back. Wee were ordered then to report to Richmond. Wee went back to Orag. C. H. and took the train. Wee landed in this cty last night and were going to Yorke Town, but thir came a telegraph Dispatch that they had pleanty of force thir. Thay ar expecting a large battle thir. I dont know whir wee will go to now. Jeff Davis is gon to Norfolk. Thay have bin fighting thir ever since Sunday. Davis has repulced the enemy 5 times. . . .

J. T. Thompson

"P.S. You said that thay were about to ride Governor Brown on a rail. I wish thay had. He is going to make us pay $2.50 for the blankets that wee bought and paid our own money for at home. Now he is Going to make us pay him for them just as if he had furnished them himself. Capt. Nunnally sayes he will suffer himself . . . before the companie shal pay anything. I would not be surprised if Wee were not in Savannah in 3 weeks, but wee dont Want to go thir if Wee can help it."[20]

☆ **IV** ☆

# "We Ar Station in 16 Miles of Richmond"

President Abraham Lincoln's pen was to change the destiny of many, including that of young James Thompson. The boy James was not to see Savannah in three weeks—or ever again.

The impatient President had made it clear to General George B. McClellan that he must bestir himself and do something immediately about overcoming the Confederate Army to satisfy a disgruntled Northern public.

Within an hour after embarking from the boat that took him to Fort Monroe, the Yankee General would have been willing to corroborate James Thompson's earlier statement, "I tell you it is trouble to moov such a large army." Seven days after Thompson's comment, on April 2, McClellan was to find out just how much trouble it was to move approximately sixty thousand men and one hundred guns over deceptive roads. But he had begun what Lincoln had demanded. He was moving his well-trained men toward Yorktown—his goal, the Confederate capital at Richmond.

Army wagons mired up to their axles; men and animals sank in the beautiful sandy roads. One officer claimed to see a mule sink out of sight, except for his ears, in the gumbo mud.[1]

In addition to superior forces and equipment on land, McClellan had the advantage of the famous ironclad *Monitor* that came steaming up the James River. Also, he had a new military device, T. S. C. Lowe's observation balloons.[2]

But in spite of his balloons, McClellan was too ready to listen to General Heintzelman who advised him it would be necessary to corduroy the boggy roads before they could reach the Confederates, who were strung out across the peninsula in their entrenchments from Yorktown on the River York to the mouth of Warwick Creek, located on the James River.

Bewhiskered Heintzelman viewed the enemy through the eyes of a pessimist, not knowing that much they had accomplished was as deceptive as the roads they had come over. Although amateur actor "Prince" John B. Magruder was able to fool Heintzelman and McClellan about his defenses, especially his "Quaker guns" made of wood, interspersed with several dozen naval guns (captured from the U. S. Navy Yard at Norfolk), he could not fool General Joseph E. Johnston when he came to make his inspection. Johnston hastily returned to Richmond to report to General Lee that Magruder was taking his play-acting too far, and that McClellan could capture him in a trap with little trouble. But McClellan sat for almost a month, while Prince John waited for action.

On the Confederate side of the river Kittrell J. Warren and the 11th Georgia had plenty to "beef" about, and everybody did with the exception of enthusiastic James who was still glorying in the life of a soldier.

The 11th Georgia had been transported from Richmond on the James River on sail boats attached to gun boats and had landed at King's Landing. From there they marched to the Confederate breast works at Dams 1, 2, and 3.[3]

Warren wrote of this march and occupation in some detail: "We struck up a double quick in the direction of Wynn's Mill, and soon reached a point at which random shells begun to whistle around us. Presently our route led in open view of the Abolition battery, stationed at Dam No. 1, which opened fire upon us with some energy, but its missiles sung harmlessly through the trees above our heads, and in a few moments we were lost to Yankee view in the contiguous forest. About five hundred yards beyond Dam No. 1, the regiment was ordered to 'halt,' 'front,' and rest in place. We had not remained in this position long before a rapid and heavy volley of musketry immediately to the left, admonished us that the battle had begun. The seventh [regiment], accompanied by Colonel [Tige] Anderson, came charging furiously by with shouts that rung audibly through the forests for miles around. Occupying the position we did, it was the duty of our regiment to have remained in the rear as a reserve for the 16th Georgia. But without waiting for a word of command the line was formed, guns loaded, and officers and men moved forward to meet the enemy. After advancing about two hundred yards we suddenly came upon and entered the rifle pits constructed by General Magruder from one end of the line to the other, where we remained during the entire evening in mud and water more than half knee deep. And now the battle begun to rage with great and increasing fury. In a locality peculiarly adapted to the transmission of sound, the shrill treble of musketry and the coarse, harsh, bass of artillery blent in mighty unison—a solemn, grand, imposing concert—an appropriate requiem for the fallen brave. Stationed along an inward curve of the pits with a wide pond stretching to the front, our position was not easily accessible to the enemy, whose lines were wholly beyond the reach of our Springfield muskets. So, with the exception of a few scattering volleys from long range guns, we bore no share in the perils of the occasion. Night, at length, ended the battle, and sent the discomfited Yankees howling back to their kennels.

"The reader will remember that, before moving out upon the line, we had been compelled to abandon our overcoats and blankets. So here we were, thoroughly wet from the knees down, with neither fires nor permission to build them, to say nothing about the absence of rations. But we managed to live through that as we have through many other such occasions since. The regiment remained along this part of the line during the balance of the month, drinking filthy water and living on barely enough rations to keep soul and body together, and they composed of beef and bread without either grease or salt. Our pits and the Yankees' were within five hundred yards of each other, and the intervening swamps afforded fine facilities for guerrila shooting, which was carried on daily, almost hourly, between the parties. A good portion of the time we occupied a position opposite Dam No. 1, where scarcely a head was raised above the embankment without being fired at."[4]

Captain Nunnally wrote his sister Molly that "The day after our arrival, the engagement of the sixteenth of April took place, in which our brigade was principally the only one in the action. I had one man wounded and none killed. We remained here in gun shot of the enemy until the fourth of May. During this time, I experienced the hardest service that I have seen since I have been in the army. We were on duty every other day and sometimes every day in the trenches up to our knees in mud, frequently without a morsel to eat for thirty-six hours, had but little sleep, occasionally shot at by the enemy. With no blankets for several days, the weather quite cool, allowed no fires. . . ."[5]

The Confederates slipped away from their enemies under cover of darkness, after waiting almost a month for McClellan to do more than skirmish. Captain Nunnally wrote of this retreat: "We left or evacuated on the night of the fourth of May. We were the last to leave, marching all night. The fight at Williamsburg came off next day. It was a very severe fight. Our regiment was not in it. We continued marching all that day to a late hour at night. You can well suppose how we welcomed sweet Morpheus, not withstanding the enemy was close upon our heels. The march on up Chickahominy River is characterized with the severest of the campaign. Marching and countermarching over the muddiest roads in the world, on one occasion do I remember one night march that the mud and water frequently came up to a man's waist. It might be said that Gen. Joe Johnston retreated from Yorktown to his base in and around Richmond in line of battle."[6]

James Thompson had great pride in his fellow Confederates, and although he admitted they had to retreat from Yorktown, he claimed they were victors in several of the "heavy fights."

"New Kent County, Va.
May the 13, 1862

"I seat myself to drop you a few lines to let you know that i am well and enjoying life better than i ever did before in my life. Wee ar station in 16 miles of Richmond. Wee fell back from York Town in order to Get the enemy out from under the cover of thir Gun boats. Thir was 7 or 8 of the Virginians desirted and went over to the Yankies, which caused the enemy to persue us rapidly on our retreat back. Wee had 3 or 4 heavy fights in which wee whiped them badly. Wee dont intend to fall back another foot, but wee intend to fan them out if wee get the chance. Wee think if Wee can giv them a good whiping hear the show will be over.

"Wee whiped them out at West Point and maid them leav their napsacks, an nearly evry one had a ham of meet and coffee a pleanty in thir napsacks.

"We taken a Great manie prisners. Some of our boyes ask the Yankies why they didnt fight better. 'What makes you runn?' Thay say 'Whoo in the hell could stand when you come with fixed bayonetts yeling as hard as you can?' Thay say that all the little Dried up Georgians knows is to fight a bayonett fight. Wee lost our napsacks and evry thing wee had, but the suit wee had on. The government will Giv us lots in a few days. When wee Got about half way between York Town and Richmond the General said that the Yankies had Got betwen us and Richmond and wee were cut off. Anderson said, 'Boyes, wee will fight our way threw with the bayonett. Wee will go threw them Damb Yankies or di in the attempt,' but the Yankies never got ahead of us. Anderson is the most cearful [careful] man i ever saw, the most watchful. He stands up to us like a father.

"In the battle of York Town the 11th was taken out of his brigaid and put under Howel[l] Cob[b] for some purpose i dont know what, and the Yankies charged on our batrie. The North Carrolinians runn. Anderson toal the 7 regment to charg Bayonetts and to recolect the batle of the 27. He went rite with them waving his hat and hallowing all the way &c. Anderson is General over the 7, 8, 9 and 11th regment. . . .

"Bob Tombs is our Major General. Anderson is our Brigadier. Old Gary our Liutenant Colonel is no count. He is like old Fowler. He is never with us. Wee hav a nomber on major. He is not afraid of nothing. He nowes how to treat his men, he nowes when his men is treated rite. While Wee were at York Town Geting only half rations Howel Cob Had meet cooked and bredd and sent to us. . . ."[7]

Kittrell Warren wrote: "On the 15th, our 'On to Richmond,' was resumed, and the lowering elements again discharged their liquid contents on the drenched and soaking earth. Having halted two nights and one day, on picket, at Middle Bridge, we marched through the environs of Richmond, and bivouacked on the 18th, three miles west of the city, on the New Meadow Bridge road.

"The season for inaction had passed," continued Kittrell, "and, like the wandering Jew, it was doomed thenceforth to be ever moving with restless, wakeful, wearying regularity. On the 21st we crossed Meadow Bridge, and having gone about a mile from the railroad, in the direction of Mechanicsville, established temporary picket posts. In the afternoon the enemy's skirmishers met our cavalry about a half mile in advance of us, and brisk firing occurred. Lt. Colonel Luffman moved the regiment to an eligible point, among some bushes in rear of a field, to the road side, and placed it in position. Here we waited for the enemy until night, when, being again disappointed, we retired beyond the railroad, recrossed the bridge and camped on Strawberry hill.

"We remained at this place guarding Meadow Bridge and other neighboring posts, until the 31st, when we began slowly to descend the Chickahominy, performing picket duty at its various crossings, and at length, on the western borders of the Seven Pines battle-field, until the 6th of June, when we quartered rather more permanently, near the residence of Mrs. Price, and immediately in rear of the Garner farm."[8]

At the end of May the Chickahominy was a raging torrent, as if in violent protest that brother should destroy brother. The Federal Army found itself astride this angry stream when Johnston ordered an attack at Seven Pines on May 31.

Seven Pines battlefield was so named by the Confederates because seven large pines grew in a clump. There were five or six thousand casualties on each side during this two-day engagement. It was here that one could hear the Louisiana Zouaves receiving their commands in French, that the Confederate wounded had to be leaned against trees to keep them from drowning and some of the Federals were burned because powder flashes set the woods afire. It was here that both armies learned that battles were not all glory, but also stench, because bodies were washed up from their shallow graves, and some were never buried, creating an unholy stench that seemed to cry up from the ground.[9]

The next day, on June 1, at nearby Fair Oaks[10] (The Yankee side of Seven Pines) the Confederates were repulsed and General Johnston was severely wounded, once in the shoulder and again in the chest. Johnston relinquished his command to Gustavus W. Smith. As a direct result, General Robert E. Lee assumed command of the Army of Northern Virginia.[11]

"The fate of Richmond now seemed pendant and trembling in doubtful scales," wrote Warren. "The 'flower' of the Northern army stood knocking at her gates. . . . To the Abolitionist soldiery the steeples of the city were already visible in the distance and being pampered, well rested and well clad, they had no doubt in performing, with ease, the long coveted pilgrimage to this Mecca of their idolatry."[12] The Federals might have disagreed that they were "pampered" and "well rested," because the Confederates had kept them so well occupied in rugged territory for the past month.

James Thompson had been busy also, and apparently there was no time to write home between May 13 and June 20, 1862. On June 20 he took his pen in hand to ask his father's permission to continue on in the army. A great many of the volunteers in the Confederate Army had completed a year's service, and as young Thompson put it, "Thay ar beating up for regulars." Thompson was still so enthusiastic about army life, in spite of Yankees, mud, water, snakes, half rations, sleeping in the rain, and all the inconvenience it must have brought him, that he asked his father's permission to enlist for six years.

"Richmond, June the 20, 1862
"Thes few lines leave mee well and sound. Hoping thay may find you all in Joying the same. I saw Uncle Seabron [Cochran] last Saturday. I was with him only a few minuts. He brought mee a letter from you. I havent much newse to tell you. I am still cooking for the companie. . . . Thay ar beating up fo regulars to sirv for six years. . . . Thay offer $100 bounty and $25 per month, and as I pride in the glory and honor of a solgers life, as nothing else suits mee better, i think I shal join. Write to mee soon what you think of it as the Confedrat Stats is obblig to have a regular army. I shant join untill i Get an answer from you. . . . Write soon for i dont want to wait long before i join. You said iff i wanted anything to let you know. . . . Thir is nothing i want but a hat, and i am Going to write to Tom Evans to hav mee one maid and sent to mee by the first one that passes. Nothing more at preasant.

J. T. Thompson
"P. S. I would have wroat more, but Uncle Sebron can tell you more than i can write to you."[13]

On June 26, General Lee took the offensive against the overly cautious McClellan. "Prince" John Magruder had been left to keep the Federals in check south of the Chickahominy River. Lee had ordered Stonewall Jackson to bring his men by rail from the Shenandoah Valley and to attack the rear and flank of Porter's corps. Jackson upset the timing of Lee's plan by being a day late.

A. P. Hill, leading the Confederate advance, attacked the Federals at Mechanicsville without Jackson's aid. The retreating Union troops battled the Confederates from trenches behind Beaver Dam Creek. The Southerners were repulsed with heavy losses.

On June 27, Lee won his first victory at the battle of Gaines's Mill; however, it was a bitter victory because the fallen were legion.

McClellan's communications with President Lincoln and his aides were so threatened that he must make a choice between moving his base to the James River, where he would have the protection of the Federal Navy, or retreat down the Peninsula. On June 28, McClellan and his Fifth Corps began their move toward Malvern Hill. They moved through White Oak Swamp. On June 29, Magruder attacked them at Savage Station, but being unaided he could not hold his ground.

On June 30, the Federals fought off the Confederates at Glendale (Frayser's Farm). For some reason, best known only to him, "Stonewall" Jackson failed to pursue the enemy, and they made their escape.[14]

It was another two weeks before Thompson was able to write home again to describe recent battles and especially to ask for food and clothing.

"2½ Miles Dwe East of Richmond
July the 15, 1862

"Dear Parents, I again seat myself to drop you a few lines to let you know that i am still uppon the stage of action. . . . I hav just got back from the City. I Went up thir yesterday Evning with Liutenant Arnold . . . to pick up straglers that runn of[f] in the time of battle. Wee only got 24. We will hav to go nearly evry day untill Wee get them all. I saw the Wrights Leagon last week. I saw Uncle Ewell Hardman. He was Well then and look very Well, but complained of being very tired. But i recon When thay all march as mutch as this Thompson has they wont complain. I had rather be marching than to be living about. I hav marched over 500 miles in the last 12 months. . . . Little Tom Carroll is at the point of death. His mother is With him, all so one of the young Tanners come with Rhody out hear. . . . Nearly all of the Gwinett boys in Bradburies Co. got wounded. Jim Carroll told mee that Uncle Ewel was sick, and Urier [Hardman] died last Wednesday at Charlottsville hospital with the measels. I recon Aunt Susan will nearly go Deranged when she hears of it. I think Urier Was one among the best boys i ever saw. . . .

"If it had not bin for Anderson in the Tusdays battle i dont know what would have become of us, for [Lieutenant] Colonel [William] Luffman left us to shift for ourselves. Both he and our Major Luffman never come to us untill next day, and the Major kept on to Richmond and resigned.[5] Wee hav Got one now i think will stand. His name is Liddell from Walker county. Anderson left his horse and took it afoot rite with us. . . . Som of the companies runn clear off. Anderson spoak out plain and publicly, 'If i cant get the regment to go with mee i will take the Walton infantry, my old companie. I know thay will go.' He says, 'Boys, stick to your colors.' Our wounded boys ar mending. . . .

"Tell Mother to make mee 2 coton shirts, 2 par of drawers, 2 or 3 par socks. I hate to bother her, but evrything is so no count and high hear that i dont want them. I would not ask her to make them if ther was any other chanc. Mother, if you please, put mee up a jug of pickels. You will hav to cut them fine so as to Get them into a jug. Thay dont do well in jares to ship this fair [far]. Put in some small peaches, cucumbers, beats, unions [onions], red pepper, and such like, if you hav them. Several of the boys of my mess ar all Ways getting such things from home and thay all Ways Divide with mee. If Father comes out he can bring them. If he dont come, Write to me when you get them ready and i will direct you how to Direct the Box. I would prefer my shirts striped and my drawers purple, and you can do as you pleas about the socks. Write to mee soon whir [whether] Father will come or not as I want to write to him before he comes. He can find somebody from Walton coming hear constant. I expect Jim Clay & Bob Guthriy will come out soon. Doctor John Barcley is hear now.

"I have to frank my letters. Wee cant get postage stamps in Richmond. The government hasnt got them at present, but will hav them soon. I recived 2 letters from you last weeke. I wroat a letter to Grandfather on the 13th of this month. I hoap he Will receiv it, for I want to hear from him."[15]

## ☆ V ☆

# "You Must Call Them the Malvin Hill Turnip"

The Federals, led by the thirty-five-year-old McClellan, retreated to Malvern Hill, near the James River. In his determination to win, General Lee attacked the enemy on July 1 in its almost impregnable position.[1] Major General D. H. Hill later described the battle of Malvern Hill dramatically in seven words, "It was not war—it was murder."

The Seven Days' battles around Richmond had cost the determined Confederates 20,000 soldiers, 3,286 of whom were killed. Both James Thompson and Captain Nunnally survived the battle of Malvern Hill, and each wrote brief versions to his family.

According to Captain Nunnally, the battle of Malvern Hill "was a most terrific battle. The enemy had thirty pieces of artillery playing on us besides their infantry, and continued from two in the evening until nine at night. After night had closed in on the scene I beheld one of the grandest views I ever witnessed. It beggars description. Imagine thirty pieces of artillery belching forth missiles of death and destruction and burning fire and bursting bombs lighting up the heavens and with it mingling the many thousand small arms and you will but get a faint idea of the grand scene.

"If you could have but heard the groans of the wounded and dying that night you would have sworn eternal vengence against the whole Yankee tribe. In the action I had two killed and six wounded. I was not touched myself during the engagements."[2]

As far as James Thompson was concerned, the battle had not been so "terrific" as to make him forget his family down in Georgia. He took time to gather some turnip and "cabag" seed. Apparently, in an effort to keep the two types of seed separate, Thompson sent them home in two letters.

"Sadurdy
August the 2nt, '62
"It is with pleasure that I seat myself to answer yours of the 20th, which came to hand yesterday. . . . We have about 100 peaces of Artilry to go down on the south side of James river, 5 miles below City Point. Thay shelled the Yankies gunn boats from 10 o'clock untill 2. This was night before last. The gunn boats sheled desperately, but to no affect. Next morning there was not a gun boat to be seen for several miles. It is the opinion of the people that Mc-Clenons Army is going to the valie for thay ar taking evry thing that the citizens has got and leaving them uppon starvation. Wee are listening for Stone Wall Jackson to hav a heavy battle up thir with them. All this part of the country looks like it was ruind. The Citizens hav all mov off and left thir wheat shocked up in the field, thir corn all in tosel. Thay hav left a heap of thir stock, furniture, and evrything to be handle[d] and be abused and distroyed just as the soldiers sees fit. . . .

"Enclosed you will find some turnip seed, larg yellow flat turnip. I want you to sow them in a good place and try to save seed. You must call them the Malvin Hill turnip, for I got them at a house near Malvin Hill battleground, whir the big battle was on Tusday. . . . I hav some Cabag seed. I will send some evry leter i write.

"The Caninadding the other night was the heaviest i eavr heard in my life, and i hav bin in whir hundreds of them wir shooting at once. I saw a slug waying over 100 pounds, 22 inch long, 8 inches in diameter. . . . Thay fairly gored the ground the other night and thay wir 8 or 10 miles off.

"Tell Granfather's girls i reciv their letter and answered

it next day. I havnt no postage stamps at preasant, or i would hav paid the postag.

"You need not talk about furlow to me, for i couldent Get one if i wanted it. Thir ant but one way that i know of, that is if old Dock Hamilton [Stone Mountain, Ga.] wants his Negro sent home next Christmas and he will write to Anderson to send him by mee, mabie i can get off. That is all the chanc i no of. You need not say anything about it untill the time comes.

"My young widow hasent wroat to mee in some time. I recon she has forgot mee. I dont cear [care] if she has.

"Write soon. I will write next week."[3]

August 30, 1862, has been described by an able historian as "one of the glorious days of the Confederacy."[4] General Stonewall Jackson, followed by Generals Lee and Longstreet and their half-hungry Confederates, made their way via Thoroughfare Gap to the old battlefield at Bull Run (Manassas). Here they repulsed the Union forces under Pope.

Warren described the part of the 11th Georgia played on this fateful day. "The morning sun ushered in the 30th of August—a sun that shone on carnage and glory; a day destined to be forever memorable in the halls of time; a sun whose dial marked the course of events which must forever rank among the most important and illustrious of history; a day whose voice will be audible to remote posterity as it discourses eloquently of patriotism and valor. . . .

"About four o'clock in the afternoon the fighting commenced. Our regiment was kept upon the qui vive in momentary expectation of being summoned to join our comrades on the field. Our expectations were soon . . . realized; acting Major General Jones came galloping up and announced that 'another Manassas victory has been gained, the enemy are in full retreat and I want everybody to join in the pursuit.'

"[It was] a scene of moral grandeur to behold that line, torn, mangled and bleeding, yet pressing onward, madly, proudly, defiantly onward; and now having travelled more than a mile in this furious hurricane, we . . . reached a thicket of under-growth, when suddenly from behind a fence, the invisible foe poured a deadly volley into our reeling ranks. New life seems imparted to the men of the regiment, and though confronted by more than five times their number, they begin their part in the terrible drama, with a zeal and earnestness which no terrors could check or abate.

"Colonel Luffman, who had been severely wounded in both legs, and able to walk only with great difficulty, still stayed with, and encouraged his men until the relief arrived, when the command devolved on Major Little. . . .

"Colonel Anderson, who was in front of us, spoke out in a clear voice. 'Men, I am going to give an order which I want executed with as much composure as if you were on battalion drill; about face, forward march,' and through woods, where scarce a tree or bush failed to bear marks of the havoc going on, the regiment preserved its alignment. Our part in the battle was now performed, for soon the tumult and commotion of the conflict gave place to loud, stentorian shouts of victory! victory! and the field was ours."[5]

"The 31st of August," continued Warren, "and 1st of September were devoted to pursuing the enemy up the Fairfax road. In the evening of the last mentioned day the regiment bivouacked on the battle field of Young's Mill, from which point, at night, they moved forward treading, as it were, upon the heels of the enemy, and receiving, in return, the contents of a battery rather copiously administered. But our line advancing as if no obstacle were before it, when we neared them they ceased firing and disappeared in the darkness. We accordingly stationed suitable pickets, and having sought a convenient position, spent the remainder of the night. . . .

"The succeeding day was appropriated to the work of drawing and cooking rations, and bringing up the unfinished business of our much abused and long neglected appetites. On the morning of the third, bright and soon we were again on the pad in search of Yankees, but they had eluded pursuit, and having marched three miles up the Alexandria road we returned, and took the Leesburg turnpike for Maryland. After going by Drainsville and through Leesburg [where the barefooted men who would consent to do so remained] we waded the Potomac ten miles above the latter place, and entered Maryland on the sixth. From thence we wound through Buckeytown, across the Monocacy river, and on towards Frederick, near which place we struck camp for two days, in order to cook, rest and recruit."[6]

During this period James Thompson was "runing about so mutch" that his mail not only couldn't catch up with him, but he appears not to have had time to write his parents until September 22, 1862, from Winchester, Virginia.

"Dear parents. . . . Wee keep runing about so mutch that the mail cant cetch up with us. Thir is mail somewhir for us. Wee will Get [it] soon. You must not Get out of hart if you dont Get no letters from me. I will write evry chance i Get. I come hear to reast awhile. Thir is 2 or 3 Hundred of us hear in camps. Wee hav marched about so mutch that wee were obliged to rest. Jackson fell back several miles this side of the Potomac in order for Johnson's army to cross over so he could rest his men. Wee had several days hard fighting to do in Meriland, but wee lost very few men. Wee Get a great manie wounded. Anderson's brigaid was in all the battles, but he never lost manie or got manie wounded. Our regment got 5 wounded, nary one killed. One man in our company slitly wounded. As soon as Jackson began to fall back the Yanks began to follow us up, but as soon as Johnson's Army got with Jackson's thay maid the Yankees lie futher. Wee hav drov them back into Meriland and our armie is again over the Potomac. I hav waided the Potomac 4 times in 3 diferent places. I am Geting very tired of wading rivers. If you Get this letter soon i wish you would take my cloth[e]s down to Monroe. Liutenant Arnold is at home. If you Get to see him send mee 1 pair pants, 2 shirts, 2 par drawers, 2 or 3 par socks, 1 par shooes. Dont bother to send nothing elce. It will be too much trouble. Send mee 25 or 30 dollars by him if you see him, for wee cant draw any money now. Thay ow us for six months wages, $25 for clothing, $50 bounty. I dont know when wee will draw. I am needing money & cloaths boath. I need cloths wors than anything elc."[7]

News of the battle at Bull Run on August 30 had elated the South. It was considered a tremendous victory for the Confederate Army.

General Robert E. Lee concluded that the hour was propitious to strike a staggering blow to the enemy by invading Maryland. The General, along with many other Southerners, felt that the defensive policy of Jefferson Davis could never win the war and restore peace to the South. A major move such as the threatening of Harrisburg and Washington appeared necessary. To move his army through Maryland, recruiting men and obtaining much-needed supplies, seemed worth the necessary risks.

Once more James Thompson and his fellow Confederates must wade another river—this time the Potomac near Leesburg. Some 50,000 soldiers of the Army of Northern Virginia crossed the water, singing "Maryland! My Maryland" and marched to Frederick.[8]

The invasion of Maryland did not go well for the South, however. The Confederates were inadequately shod, and such food as they could provide for themselves caused diarrhea. This intestinal disturbance was aggravated by the eating of green apples and green corn. The populace looked upon the invaders with a hostile eye, and Lee failed to gain the recruits for his weakened army that he had hoped for,[9] despite his strict orders that his men must respect the property of the citizens along their route.

Captain Nunnally described the Maryland expedition in a long letter: "On the 12th of August, just before the break of day, we got aboard the cars for Gordonville on the famous expedition into Maryland. We left Gordonville in pursuit of Pope who then was at Culpepper [*sic*] C. H. We came upon them in the night at Racoon Ford on the Rapid Ann [Rapidan]. We waded the river some two or three hundred yards wide and waist deep with trepidation of the heart for we expected every moment the Yankee batteries to open on us from the heights on the opposite side but to our great satisfaction we found crossing that they had fled. The weather was cool and with our clothing wet and in line of battle with fire we spent the night. Horrible night it was, no sleep that night and marched all next day, a distance of over twenty miles. After marching and countermarching for several days and nights we came upon the enemy upon the banks of the Rappahannock River at the railroad station. They were on one bank and we on the other. We lay out in an open field from nine in the morning until four in the evening, the weather being very warm, under one of the severest shellings of the war. I could see distinctly the enemy as he would pull the lanyard to the cannon that was to throw the missile of death into our ranks, I could see bombs as they come, I could see men on my right and left fall victims to their deadly shots and we could inflict no injury on them whatever. We had to lay motionless hugging our mother earth as we would hug our sweethearts. At four we withdrew, the enemy firing at us as we marched out. We had to march near a mile under fire, I had one killed, R. M. Preston and three wounded. Bro. Joe was slightly wounded here. It was not the object of our Genl. to fight at this point we being thrown out to cover other movements of the army.

"We cooked rations that night, all we had or would get. Next day we marched up the Rappahannock several miles and listened to whistling bombs that evening on its banks, no one hurt from my command; camped at this place that night crossed over some six miles above. Next day marched to a late hour that night, slept without rocking, but considerably worried until we reached Thoroughfare Gap, a mountain pass for the Va. Central Road. Here we came up with the Yankees again. They were posted on the right and left of the pass. There were two ways by which they were accessible which were down the railroad or over the mountains. We went the former until we were fired upon and then we filed to the left and scaled the mountain after them. This was done with but little loss to our forces. The mountain was covered over with a very dense shrubery [*sic*], and we succeeded in dislodging the enemy just at dark and some of my men went over this thicket after night barefooted. We rested on the enemies' side of the remainder of the night, next morning bright and early we took up line of march to the memorable plains of Manassas.

"We reached that place in the evening, heavy fighting was going on at the time. We were carried into our positions under a very heavy artillery fire. We failed to get into the engagement that day, but the next day, the 31st of Aug. 1862 we met them. The roar of the artillery and the bursting of bombs made the earth tremble beneath us. I must acknowledge that I never was in an engagement so terrible as this. We marched up in forty yards of their lines under a very severe fire. A fence separated us which the Yankees held; we held our position until thirty out of forty of my command were killed or wounded. I had ten killed out of this number on the field. We [were] then ordered back. We fell back some two or three hundred yards in good order, being relieved by another command. We remained here but a few moments when we were ordered back. When we started back to meet them I looked at my company and Oh! what a sad thought flashed over me, out of forty brave and gallant soldiers only ten were left to follow up the retreating foe, and a still sadder thought occured [*sic*] to me when I thought who were among the gallant dead and wounded. Who filled the list of dead, who filled the list of the wounded? These were questions that I feared an answer, but they thrust themselves upon me and I could but learn who they were. Ten were killed and twenty wounded, among the latter was young Bro. Joe, of whom you as well as myself should be proud, for he has acted most valorous in every engagement he has been in. The fight closed soon after night fall, the enemy continuing to fall back. We rested on the battle field that night, doing but little else than collecting the wounded. We left early next morning in pursuit of the fleeing foe, leaving behind quite a small detail to care for wounded and bury the dead. Next day we came upon him just after a sharp skirmish of our advance guard in the vicinity of Fairfax Court House. We halted here, cooked rations and then turned in the direction of Leesburg on the Potomac.

"Within three nights from this time we slept upon the banks of the Great Stream. Early in the morning we were aroused and ordered to the ford known as White's. We stripped our pants and drawers and plunged into its beautiful waters. This was a grand sight, both novel and exciting; novel because of the peculiar view presented by nature's uniforms; exciting because we were crossing into Maryland. I knew not for what point we were bound, some supposed Baltimore, others the Relay House, some that we were going into Pennsylvania, etc. But [on] the second day's march we reached Frederick City on the Ohio and Baltimore R.R. We destroyed at this place one of the finest structures of a bridge I ever saw. We remained here two days and left for Hagestown [Hagerstown], that is, Longstreet's Corps, while Jackson went to Harper's Ferry.

"We remained two days at Hagestown (here I was taken quite sick, nausea, living on green apples and corn, but little else to eat) when we were ordered back to Boonsborough to a gap in the mountains known as Crampton Gap in double quick time, as the enemy was making a desperate effort to carry the Gap in order to save the garrison at Harper's Ferry, which was then being stormed by the forces of Gen. Jackson. Longstreet's Corps arrived in time to hold the point until Jackson had accomplished his object at the Ferry. Our forces then fell back to Sharpsburg, three miles from the Potomac, the enemy pursuing.

"At this point we were joined by Gen. Jackson's forces after he had caused a surrender of Harper's Ferry with eleven thousand prisoners and as many small arms, ninety pieces of artillery and equipments also all of their camp and garrison equipage, etc. It was on the sixteenth of September that he joined Longstreet. On the 17th, the bloodiest [battle] that ever was fought on this continent was fought in and around this little town in Maryland. We met the enemy who with twice our number fought us all that day and to [a] late hour that night, neither party getting the better of the other.

"The fight was not renewed next day, except slight skirmishing. That night we recrossed the Potomac at Sheperdstown, Va. (wading) in the face of the enemy, he being so badly crippled that he dare not to follow us. [We left] our wounded and dead on the field. Some days after, a division of the enemy crossed over in pursuit of us, as we were then resting very quietly at Martinsburg, Va. They were jumped upon by our forces and who completely demolished them. It was said that the Potomac was bridged over with the dead bodies of the Yankees and that the stream appeared as a river of blood.

"I sufficiently recovered from my wounds and sickness to join my command at Martinsburg, Va. We remaind [sic] here but a short while and fell back to Winchester, Va."[10]

At Winchester James Thompson finally caught his breath long enough to sit down and write his loved ones a letter.

"Near Winchester, Virginia
October the 1st, 1862

"I seat myself to answer the 3 letters that i received from you & the Girls. Our mail reached us on the 29th inst. I received 6 letters. The latest newse that i hav from home is the letter that Elizabeth [his sister] wroat to mee mailed Sept. the 2nt. Tell her & the others that i will write to them next week. . . . Our Companie is recruiting very fast. The boys ar coming in from the Hospitals that hav bin off sick. Dick Easley come in yesterday from the hospital. He had [a] very tight spell of feaver for 6 weeks. . . . The Companie is about 50 strong at this time besids the wounded boys. Thay ar all gon home. The sick boys keeps coming in evry day.

"Wee onely had 16 to represent the big fight in Meriland. Wee just whiped them out completly hear. When wee fell back out of Md. across the river "Uncle Stone Wall" lay s[t]ill untill the Yankies all got over on this side then he picked into them and just slaughtered them and while thay were wading the river trying to Get back into Meriland ... wee runn Artilry upon the bank & Throwed Grape shot and canister among them, so the river was completely damed up and so thick with blood that the river looked like blood for miles below. This has bin since the leter i wroat to you last week. You can tell the boys that thay may brag on John Morgan, but he cant come up with "Uncle Stone." Tell them he dont Get behind stumps & trees as thay say thay did. We hant got the trees & stumps to Get behind. Thay say he is like a flee. When thay think thay have got him fast & go in to get him out, he is clear Gon & is whiping them somewhir elce. Some of the boys swares "Stone Wall" can kick up the Devil in 5 minuts any time. It dose look like he can hav a fight just when he Gets ready.

"You say Morgan is taring up Kentucki. I think he is wrong for distroying the country. When wee went into Meriland wee dident burn a pear of rails or pull a apple or rosineer [roasting ear] without leaf [permission] from the oaner. Wee were in 2½ miles of the Pencilvania line, rite among Unionest. Wee dident say anything out of the way to anybody. Thay said that wee done better than thir one [own] people. Over in Meriland is the best country for stock and Grain that i ever saw. I saw wheat stacks 3 years old, corn better than any bever rain i ever saw, & thay said thay wire onley making half crops of corn. If thay wir to make whole crops i dont know what thay would do with it. Thir is noth[ing] making in this part of Virginia. It has bin two dry. Thir hasent bin no rain in 2 months of a count. Wee had 2 heavy frost las week.

"I dident stay at Winchester but a few days before i wanted to Go back to the camp. Wee are in 6 miles of Winchester cooking up 3 days rations. Our wagons ar gon on towards Richmond.... Wee will hav to come back on the railroad so wee can Get supplies. Wee will hav to Get close to the railroad, for when the rains commencis wee cant hawl or carry Artilry about. I understand it is reported at home that i hav joined the regulars. It is falce. I dont intend to join them. I think your advis on that subject very good. I shall take it anyhow. . . .

"You said you was seling off all the stock you could spar. I think it a good idea. . . ."[11]

## ☆ VI ☆

# "You Wanted to Know If I Am Under 'Stone Wall' or Not. I Am."

When James wrote to his family about his commander, Stonewall Jackson, his pen portrait of Lee's most able corps commander was not physically flattering, but his admiration for, and confidence in this man was equal to that of any soldier in the original famous Stonewall Brigade. One can see in imagination the glow of pride on young Thompson's suntanned face as he penned the comment to his father, "you can tell the boys that thay may brag on John Morgan, but he can't come up with 'Uncle Stone.'"

Jackson had been given many nicknames, among them "Tom Fool" Jackson," "Old Blue Light," "Lemon Sucker," "Mountain Fox," and "The Wagon Hunter," because he had captured so many Union Army wagons, but none of these had expressed the affection of Thompson's sobriquet, "Uncle Stone."[1]

As James Thompson hastily scribbled his first brief note to his loved ones back home after the battle of Bull Run, one can see him wet his knife-trimmed pencil against his tongue, and bear down just a little harder as he added the passionate comment, "All i want is a crack at a Yankey Boy." But one senses that as time passed his anger against the "Black Republicans" with their high-handed ways was not uppermost in his thinking. Rather anger was overshadowed by a boyish hero worship of his leaders, as he still gloried in the "pride and honor of a solgers life."

"Camp near Winchester, Va.
October the 5th, 1862

"I again seat myself to answer yours of the 22nd of Sept., which came threw in 5 days. . . . I was Glad to hear from you all. Thes lines leavs mee Well and hartier than i ever was. . . .

"I saw one of Braid's companies the other day. He told mee that Braid was ether killed or a prisner. Old Cob[b] runn them down a mountain rite into the Yankies, then ordered them to retreat. When it was all most imposible, thay had to crawl up the mountain and the Yankies shooting them out like squirls. Thay sed the last thay saw of Braid him and about 16 more of the companie were fixing bayonets. Sed thay would fight till thay died before thay would runn. So i recon he is ded or a prisner. Evrything is quite [quiet] hear at preasant. . . .

"You wanted to know if i was under 'Stone Wall' or not. I am. He is a sorry looking chance. He is a little old drid [dried] up looking man [who] puts mee more in the mind of Arter Leetch in his life time than anybody elce, only he is an older man.

"You said you & Numan [Pounds—next door neighbor] was buying up stuff to sell. You had better watch, or the Government will put a price on everything and you will loose. Tell Bud Kelly to watch his money, for thir is pleanty of people hear wont take Comfedrat. Thir is some Unionist hear that refuses, but wee send them to old Jeff. . . .

"You said your horse was ded that you swaped for Dickses. He will sell you his young horse for $150, but if i was you i would get mules. Thay eat less and do better sirvis, or at least thay do in the armie.

"You said you was afraid that i was bare footed on some of thes long marches. I have got good shoos. I Got them from Liut. Burson the day before wee left Richmond. He had an extry pair he let mee hav or i should hav bin bare footed. Thir is pleanty of lawyers and Doctors hear barefooted and nearly necked that used to ware broad cloth and wouldent hardly speek to a common man. Old Sim Smith's son David, the gred [great] teacher, is in just such a fix now, and he cant help himself, but i dont say Smith is one of them fopish kind. I all ways liked Smith mity well and took him to be one among the finest young men in the county. Just write to let you know how solgers fairs hear. I dont say it because i hav anything against him at all. I feell very sorry for him, and if it was in mi power i would Giv him shooes & cloth[e]s, but our cloths and money will be hear next week. Did you have my shooe heeles irned or not? Shooes last me as long again when the heels ar irned. I wrote to you to have them done. Shooes is worth from $12 to $15 a pair in Richmond. I will come to a close for this time. I will write again as soon as the Capt. Gets his trunk. I have 3 quires of good paper in it.

J. T. Thompson"[2]

It is unlikely that James Thompson had the pleasure of wearing his new shoes, with or without irons, or using the stationery; he died less than a month later, November 1, 1862, from smallpox.

On October 16th Captain Matthew Talbot Nunnally had been sent to Richmond on business for Company H. As he was suffering from battle fatigue, he was granted a furlough, which enabled him to visit his Georgia home and procure supplies for his company.[3]

When Nunnally's furlough was at an end and he returned to the rugged life of a soldier, he was probably as willing as the youthful and exuberant James Thomas Thompson had ever been to have a final crack at a "Yankey Boy" and write *'Finish'* to a war that was keeping him away from those he loved best. On returning to camp the Captain learned some distressing news which he passed along to his sister Molly and her husband Mark, "To my regret I learned that since I left . . . two of my men had died with smallpox."[4] One of these was the uncomplaining James Thompson.

"We occupied one bank of the river and the Yankees

the other, but with little transpiring exciting until the eleventh of December," confided Nunnally to his sister and brother-in-law. "Early that morning we were drawn up in fighting attention; we knew what for because the loud peals of artillery thunder warned us what was coming. We took our position in line of battle, snow on the ground, the weather very cold. Slept that night, if sleep we did, on our arms without fires and but one blanket to the man. That night the enemy had finished throwing their pontoons across the river and had considerable force.

"The twelfth passed off with no general engagement, the thirteenth came quite misty but bearing the news from the signs that the great day had dawned. Our division early in the morning advanced some mile and a half and took position but little ways from the enemies lines. Each line being visable to both and the pickets still nearer each other; our position was good and we dared them advance feeling confident of success. But better wisdom dictated for them than to advance on that part of the line, but the pickets amused themselves throughout the day by interchanging shots.

"At nine in the morning the fight opened with great fury on the right and left, from my position I could see the engagement on the left. I saw as many as three Yankee lines advance slowly and steadily with colors flying and in beautiful battle array.... Soon our brave boys told them where the Rocks of Gibralter were; our artillery ploughed through their ranks cutting down whole platoons at a single shot, our musketry killed them by hundreds. I saw Commanders of Regts. and Brigades with dashing steeds and waving sabres leading their command onward. I saw horses run out riderless, and lastly, though not with colors flying, I saw the last line in retreat pass out of sight.

"Then [came] a yell from our side that made the very earth tremble. The day was over on that part of the line. I could not see the engagement on our left, but it was no less furious than on our right. It is said that the enemy made breast works of their dead. The fight lasted until three in the evening.

"Our loss is estimated 2500, [the] enemies 30,000. They did not renew the attack the next day, nor the next, as our Generals expected. But on the next day they had all disappeared from the south side of the Rappahannock, taking the night to recross.

"We moved back to our old camps bouyant with victory and with the hope Gen. Burnside would try us again at the same point. Since the fight we have fixed up quite comfortably for the winter knowing that the Yankees could not drive us from our position. So we sit quite easy under our tent flies, eat our bread and beef, and smoke our pipes with the happy smile of peace for a while at least."[5]

## ☆ VII ☆

# "We Lost One of Our Best Generals— That Matchless Stonewall Jackson"

When Lieutenant Henry D. McDaniel returned to Virginia after his enlistment campaign in Walton County in the fall of 1861, in which he had hoped to recruit enough men to replace the members of Company H who had sickened with measles, pneumonia, and the other diseases that were the scourge of the Confederate Army, he brought back with him seventeen-year-old William Thomas Laseter.[1] William, the son of Joel and Foriba Jeils Laseter who lived near Walnut Grove, was probably already acquainted with James Thomas Thompson who had often visited in Walnut Grove with his horse Messenger.

It was William Laseter who completed the story of life in camp with Company H after the death of James Thompson and his beloved Captain, M. T. Nunnally. In simple conversational style, Laseter wrote of the Company's last days many years later for the *Shreveport Journal*.

"It was but a short time until the enemy came up the valley, and we had a fight with them and drove them back across the Potomac river, and then our command was sent down the Strawsburg [sic] Valley, and stayed there for some time, and then we were ordered across the Blue Ridge mountain, over to the Shenandoah Valley, and from there we went to Fredericksburg and got there a few days before the first Fredericksburg fight.

"Longstreet's Corps occupied the center of the army and

we were not in the hardest of the battle. The hardest fighting was on our right and left, and it was a hard-fought battle. It was in the month of December, 1862, and then we went into winter quarters. . . ."

After Fredericksburg General James Longstreet enjoyed some of the freedom of an independent command, although he was under the direct supervision of the War Department. He had proved he was a skilled leader of men as a corps commander.

To preserve the life line of Lee's troops in case Richmond was threatened via North Carolina, on February 18 Lee, prodded by Jefferson Davis, detached Longstreet's troops from the Rappahannock. The people of Richmond breathed a little easier as Longstreet's battle-hardened men marched through their city, their mission to protect the Southern Capital and recoup diminishing supplies.

On March 17, after having been as far south as Tarborough, North Carolina, on a foraging trip, Longstreet was in Petersburg, ready to start for the Blackwater and the enemy, but Lee discouraged this. On the 18th Longstreet was back in Richmond, at which time he turned his mind to the threat against Wilmington. On March 20 Petersburg was iced in with ten to twelve inches of snow, and the mercury dropped below zero; however, the resultant bad weather did not deter Longstreet in his foraging activities. Food supplies for men and animals were necessary if they hoped to win the war against a well-fed, well-equipped, and a large-numbered adversary.

In April, Longstreet pushed along toward Suffolk, which he enveloped, but did not subdue. The road from Suffolk[2] to Norfolk became his, as well as the roads to Petersburg. Toward the middle of April he wrote Secretary of War Seddon that he had stopped firing on Suffolk as it was costing too much ammunition. Gathering supplies was more important, unless the *Richmond* could sail down the James and give him some help by blocking the mouth of the Nansemond. Union forces in Suffolk were growing more restless, and were making more aggressive local attacks. This gave Longstreet the impression that the James River would be the approach of the Yankees when they began their advance on Richmond. Longstreet ordered all the wharves and landing places along the James destroyed as a precautionary measure. The enemy was also stirring in the spring sunshine along the Rappahannock.

A startled Longstreet learned on April 30 by wire that his days of foraging and threatening Suffolk were at an end. Hooker had begun his grand offensive and Lee advised the War Department that he needed the immediate help of Longstreet, French, and D. H. Hill.

Longstreet had planned to gather supplies for two weeks longer, and his disappointment was great that he could not continue his important activities. His major problem was how to protect those supplies from the enemy, for in the words of the boy Thompson, "I tell you it is trouble to moov such a large army," and a slow process across the Blackwater into the storehouses at Richmond. Lee expected Longstreet to be in Richmond by May 2, but the War Department had failed to so advise him.

There was sharp skirmishing on May 3 in Longstreet's rear, as he crossed the Blackwater. He was defended by French's four thousand men against much greater Union numbers. Longstreet and his staff were in Petersburg by May 5, as he had left the safe loading of the supplies on rail cars at Ivor in the hands of his senior subordinate. Longstreet reached the War Department in Richmond on May 6, ready to be of assistance to Lee.[3]

Laseter wrote in the *Shreveport Journal*, "We were ordered back to General Lee at Chancellorsville. We came within one day's march of getting there in time to be in the battle, and it was there we lost one of our best generals—that matchless Stonewall Jackson."[4]

On May 21, Longstreet indiscreetly wrote D. H. Hill from near Fredericksburg, disclosing Lee's plan to cross the Potomac and meet the enemy in his own territory. While these activities were taking place the Confederacy was being lost by Pemberton, who needed help at Vicksburg.

While Longstreet was transferring his supplies, the battle of Chancellorsville had taken place and Stonewall Jackson had been fatally wounded by one of his own men. The boy Thompson had been spared the shock and bitter disappointment of knowing that his beloved "Uncle Stone" had fallen.

After Stonewall Jackson's death a reorganization took place in the Army of Northern Virginia. Longstreet retained his First Corps, less R. H. Anderson's division. The Third, a new corps, was formed from Anderson's division which was put under the command of D. H. Hill, who had been promoted to the rank of lieutenant general. Ewell was promoted to the same rank and assumed command of the Second Corps.[5]

To offset an attack by Hooker on Richmond, Lee and his lieutenants planned an attack on the industrial area of Pennsylvania where foodstuffs were plentiful. This they hoped would cause President Lincoln to call for the removal of troops to defend Washington, and then Lee could move into the rich farm area of Maryland and southern Pennsylvania.

All the South needed to gain support from England and Napoleon III was another Chancellorsville. Lee hoped Pennsylvania was the answer. Vicksburg and the west could take care of themselves, led by Pemberton and Hood.

Longstreet was to hold Hooker while Ewell, his command divided in two columns, was to march up the Cumberland Valley into Pennsylvania—one column via Williamsport toward Hagerstown, Chambersburg, and Harrisburg, the other to proceed from Sharpsburg through Emmitsburg to Gettysburg, with final destination Wrightsville, where the main highway bridge crossed the Susequehanna.

When Longstreet had routed Hooker, A. P. Hill with his Third Corps was to cross in the rear of Longstreet, passing down the Shenandoah Valley and then into Maryland. Longstreet was to cover all the gaps and passes of the Blue Ridge and to keep his troops between Hooker and the main Confederate Army.

By the eighth of June, Longstreet was at Culpeper, followed by Ewell, and Hill was at Fredericksburg. Longstreet kept Hooker's reconnaissance parties at bay; however, this Federal curiosity caused some delay because Lee was not anxious to take on Hooker's entire force.[6]

Laseter remembered that "In June we broke camp and started on the march for Gettysburg. Part of the army got to Gettysburg on the first day of July and the fighting commenced on that day. Longstreet's Corps was on a forced march all day and night of the first, and got to Gettysburg on the morning of the second day of July, and as soon as we were placed in position on the extreme right of Lee's line, our brigade was in Hood's division. As soon as we got in line we were ordered forward, and when we got to the Emmittsburg road we met the enemy, just to the right of the brick house and orchard. We drove the enemy back to the Devil's Den and so we were driving them through the Den it was there Capt. M. T. Nunley [Nunnally] was killed and others of our company, and several wounded, but, we continued to drive them until we drove them through the Den to the little roundtop mountain, and drove them to the foot of the big mountain, and then night overtook us and we could not go any further, so we fell back a short distance and straightened out our line and stayed there until next morning, and buried our dead and looked after our wounded. On that day, July 3, and the third day's fight we occupied our line all the morning with some picket fighting and cannonading.

"In the afternoon, just before General Pickett made his famous charge on the enemy line, the artilery on both sides opened up an artilery duel, and it seemed as if every piece of artillery on both sides was engaged, and during this time the Yankee cavalry on our extreme right was driving our cavalry back, and as our division (Hood's) occupied our extreme right, so our regiment, the Eleventh Georgia, and the Ninth Georgia of General Anderson's brigade was ordered to the right to reinforce our cavalry and during this time when General Pickett was making the famous charge and when we met our cavalry falling back they were fighting the enemy for every inch of ground. We had formed in line of battle and cavalry fell back over us. Then we charged the enemy and drove them back through a body of woods and when they came to an open field they surrendered, for we were right on them, and it was after sundown and the fighting ended. In our company John Arnold was killed and Billy Wiley was seriously wounded, and some others slightly wounded, and I want to say Major Henry D. McDaniel was in command of our regiment the day before Colonel Little and Lieutenant Colonel Luffman both were wounded, so the command of our regiment devolved on Major McDaniel.

### Captain Is Killed

"Billy Wiley was so critically wounded, Lieut. J. W. Morrow, who was in command of our company after Captain Nunley [Nunnally] was killed the day before [July 3, 1863], had me detailed to see Wiley back to the field hospital and I stayed there all night and helped wait on our wounded. That night General Lee gave orders to the army to fall back towards Virginia, so the Yankee army lay still and saw our army march off and made no effort to follow our army at that time."[7]

Douglas Southall Freeman listed three basic reasons why the South lost the battle of Gettysburg: (1) faulty coordination of Lee's army after the death of Stonewall Jackson, (2) inadequate supply and an (3) extended line of battle.[8] However, General James Longstreet would in years to come carry a large share of the blame for defeat at Gettysburg, which historians would refer to as "Longstreet's lack of cooperation," at the most decisive battle of the war.

Sixty-eight thousand Confederates had invaded Pennsylvania with high hopes of defeating the enemy led by General George G. Meade. It was a saddened General Robert E.

Lee who realized that his exuberant Confederates were no match for the Yankees on Northern soil, especially since there was only sufficient ammunition left for one day's fighting. Thus had come his decision to return to Virginia, after conferring with the group of Confederate leaders who had gathered at his headquarters on July 4.

After the conference with Lee, General Longstreet walked back to his headquarters with an unusual visitor, Lt. Col. James Arthur Lyon Fremantle of the Coldstream Guards, England, a military expert. General Longstreet explained to Colonel Fremantle his feeling regarding the danger of an advance immediately following Picket's charge, and explained to his visitor the steps he had taken to prevent a further disaster. At that time James Longstreet placed no blame on Lee for the failure at Gettysburg, as he would do in later years when he, Longstreet, was under heavy fire of criticism.

On July 4 some of the Confederates began an orderly retreat in a downpour of rain, while in Vicksburg the Confederates had been forced to surrender. Laseter remembered the Confederate retreat after Gettysburg and commented: "Our wagon and ambulance trains were ordered back over the same way we went to Gettysburg, so as the army was not falling back I did not know where my company was. I went back with our wagon trains to Williamsport. We had a detachment of cavalry to guard our wagon trains and on the day we got to Williamsport there was a command of Yankee cavalry which overtook us and got into our wagon trains and cut down a few wagons, so there were others, like my self, cut off from their commands, and we reinforced our cavalry and drove them back and saved our wagon trains until we got to Williamsport.

"It had been raining a good deal for some time and the Potomac river was so high it could not be forded and we had to stop in Williamsport, and then late that evening the enemy was reinforced and made another attack upon us. Every one that could handle a gun, including the drivers of the teams, went to the ordnance wagons and got arms and ammunition and we joined our cavalry and drove the enemy clear off and saved our wagon and ambulance trains. The next morning our quartermaster department received orders to send supplies to our army at Hagerstown and Funston, Md. So went back with our wagons and found my company at Funston, and in a short time after I got to my company the enemy advanced on us and we had a very hard fight for the time it lasted. That was when Major McDaniel was wounded, and Sergeant Sebe Hester and Billie Baxley was killed and some few slightly wounded.

"I was shot between my hip and cartridge box, but the bullet did not cut the skin on me. I was near Major McDaniel when he was wounded, and caught him and did not let him fall to the ground and I helped carry him off the battle field, Funkstown, Md. [July 10, 1863]. We got him on an ambulance and carried him back to the doctor's headquarters and they dressed his wounds, and it was thought by the doctors he would be able to be transferred by ambulance back across the Potomac river, but they got him as far back as Hagerstown, and then he could not be carried any further, and he was left in charge of one of our doctors to fall into the hands of the enemy, so when he got well enough he was placed in prison and was kept there until the close of the war, and they would never exchange him.

### River Is Bridged

"During this time," Laseter pointed out, "General Lee got the pontoons bridged across the Potomac river and we crossed over into Virginia, went into camp at Bunker's Hill, and then [I] was taken sick with fever and was sent to a hospital at Lynchburg and my father came to me and stayed until I got well enough to travel. . . . I was not with my company any more until the fall of 1863."[9]

The crossing into Virginia, under the supervision of General Longstreet, was not as simple as Laseter made it sound. The rain came down in blinding sheets in the black night. Torch bearers had difficulty keeping their lights aflame while helping the wounded to safety. As the lightning lighted the scene of a swollen river surging against wet banks, one could see wounded men washed into the angry waters. Men broke ranks to rescue those too helpless to save themselves. On the morning of July 13 the Confederates were relieved that the enemy had apparently slept during the night and left them to make the dangerous crossing without interference.

The line of retreat was through the Shenandoah Valley. Meade moved via Harper's Ferry and attempted to intercept Lee's muddy soldiers. The race between Meade's men and Lee's weary Confederates ended on July 24 with Longstreet occupying Culpeper Courthouse. Lee would again play a defensive role behind the Rappahannock.[10]

While Laseter was recuperating from his wound, Longstreet's men met the enemy—a large detachment of Federals having forced a crossing of the Rappahannock while on a reconnaissance mission at Kelly's Ford. Stuart's cavalry was on picket duty there, and Longstreet sent up infantry support.

Lee took up a new defensive position behind the Rapidan in early August and the Confederates busied themselves reorganizing and re-equipping for coming engagements with the enemy.

Toward the end of August, General Lee reported to Richmond, and General Longstreet was left in command.[11]

Supplies, including whiskey, were in good supply and enlivened the battle-weary Confederates. A few new recruits were also added to their ranks.

"In the fall," Laseter continued in the *Shreveport Journal*, "Longstreet was ordered from Virginia to Chickamauga. Our brigade was left at Charleston, S. C. to relieve a brigade that was put in our place; so our brigade was not in the Chickamauga fight; but so soon as the fight was over we were ordered back to take our place in the division. I got back to my company just as Longstreet was starting on the march to Knoxville. That was after my furlough expired. Our command met up with Burnside and drove him back to his breastworks at Knoxville and kept him there for some time, until General Bragg fell back from Missionary Ridge. Then General Sherman sent reinforcements to relieve Burnside, so we were forced to fight Burnside in his fortifications, but we could not drive him out.

"We had two killed in our company and several wounded. We fell back to the Holstein river, to Beene Station, and the Yanks followed us. We met up with Morgan's cavalry and then we crossed over the Holstein river to Morristown and we found out there was a force of the enemy at Strawsburg Plains, so we went for them and had quite a skirmish with them and drove them off. We went into winter quarters at Morristown and had the coldest weather I ever experienced, and on the morning of January 3 [1864] there was a detail call for seven men to go out over the country to gather up beef cattle for the army. Our command stayed in winter qaurters until the latter part of March; they then went to a place called Bull's Gap, near Greenville, Tenn., and stayed there until the last of April. Then General Longstreet was ordered back to Virginia, to join General Lee. I never saw my company but once from the time I was detailed untill I got to them the last of April in Virginia. They were on the march, going to General Lee at the Wilderness—the Wilderness fight commenced on May 5, and we got to Lee on the morning of May 6.

"Longstreet's Corps was marching right in front. General Fields' division was on the right of our Corps, and Gen. G. T. Anderson's brigade was on the right of Field's division. The Eleventh Georgia regiment was on the right of Anderson's brigade, so that put us in front of Longstreet's corps. We were marching on the plank road, going in the direction of Fredericksburg, and just as day was dawning we got to Lee's line of battle where he fought the evening before until dark, and the two armies lay there facing each other. General Hill's Corps was occupying this part of the lines, and as daylight came on the enemy advanced on Hill's line and Hill's men commenced to fall back, just in front of us. We, the Eleventh Georgia regiment, was ordered right flank off the plank road into line of battle, and just as half of our regiment cleared the road, with Company H in the center of our regiment, Hill's men fell back on us and the enemy followed, and we were ordered to fire on them which checked them, and we commenced to drive General Grant's left with our right and continued to until our corps occupied the entire right of the plank road, and a wilderness it was. We never saw any opening except where there was a right-of-way for a railroad that had been cut a few years before, so there could not be any artillery used on either side. The enemy would every now and then make a stand until we would fall back.

"This kept up until somewhere about 4 o'clock in the afternoon, when General Longstreet was wounded. That checked us until we got some one to take command. Just at the time Longstreet was wounded we were getting in sight of the opening of the river and while we were waiting for orders to go forward the enemy got a battery in position in that opening and also got reinforcements in front of us, and when we got orders to go forward and got up and started that battery opened up on us and the first shell exploded right in front of our company, and I was wounded. My command thought I was killed and passed on and left me. I was reported dead for three mornings at roll call, before they found out I had been carried off the battle field. When I came to myself to know anything I was lying on my back and was bleeding from my head, but I found out it was my nose and mouth that were bleeding, then I tried to get up on my feet but could not.

"My comrades told me afterwards that the piece of shell tore the breeching of my gun all to pieces and if it had not been for the gun it probably would have torn my right leg off. The litter bearers came along and carried me back to the rear and after the doctors dressed my wound I was sent to the hospital at Richmond and Lee and Grant kept fighting from there on down to Richmond and Petersburg. I got well and was discharged from the hospital on the Fourth of July and got to my command that day. They were at Petersburg and were occupying part of the hill where Grant blew up Lee's line afterwards. Our lines were so close together we could not have pockets or videttes in front. We occupied this position for some time. We would be relieved every other night and stay two days and nights for about three weeks, and there was firing on this part of our line day and night. We had one man killed and some wounded at this place.

### Picket Fighting Occurs

"Then we were moved further to the right, where our lines were not so close together. We had some picket fighting occasionally at this place. Just before Grant blew up Lee's line at the center to weaken it at Petersburg, Grant sent a force across the James river below Richmond to make an attack on that place, and Longstreet's corps was sent to Richmond to meet the enemy. They captured Fort Harrison and a part of our breastworks before we could get there, and the next morning after we got there we were ordered to retake Fort Harrison. We were not able to retake it, however, so Lee had another line of breastworks built and straightened out, which made our line shorter. The enemy made another flank movement on our left below Fort Harrison, and we met them at Deep Bottom and had a very hard fight and drove them back. That was when our orderly sergeant, Dick Early [Easley?] was killed, and one of the Milton boys, and several were wounded, and that was the place where we had to fight some negroes, and we surely cleaned them up. Then later on the enemy made another flank movement on our left and got possession of some of our old breastworks that we had in the Seven Days' fighting below Richmond in 62, so we attacked them out and back to their own breastworks under the protection of their gunboats on the river.

"It was in this fight that our color bearer, Seabe Tuck, was wounded, and then one of his guard was wounded, and then the third man took them and was killed, right by my side, and as there was no other guard to take them, I caught them and did not let them fall to the ground and carried them on until just as we were driving the enemy back into their breastworks, I was wounded, shot through the left arm. I will state that Company H was the center company of our regiment and the flag was always at the foot of our company. I was one of the youngest and smallest members of our company and that was my place also. I was sent to the hospital in Richmond. My wound got on fine and soon was well and when I went back to my command they were occupying our main line on the Darby Town road, below Richmond. We occupied this line of breastworks until we had to give up Richmond and Petersburg the next spring. There was about five miles of our breastworks to our left that was not occupied except about half way on the Charles City road leading to Richmond. We had a fort with twelve guns and a battalion of cavalry stationed there. The last of November the enemy made an attempt to flank us and capture the fort and get in to Richmond that way, but it was found out soon enough for us to beat them a little to the place and we gave them a good thrashing and captured over 1,100 prisoners mostly Germans. After this, on the east side of the James river below Richmond, we only had picket duty to do and occasionally a little picket fighting on some part of our lines.

"After Sherman went through Georgia and got into South Carolina and sent reinforcements to Grant at Petersburg, then Grant began to extend the lines and General Lee could not get any reinforcements, so he had to begin to stretch his lines to face Grant. On our part of the line there was only one man for every four or five spaces, and when Grant broke Lee's line at Petersburg our corps was ordered to Petersburg to reinforce Lee so he could recapture his line. When we got up to Richmond our brigade and some others of Field's division was loaded on flat cars and started a little after dark for Petersburg. After we were gone General Lee sent orders to General Longstreet not to come to Petersburg, but to go in a different direction. Lee saw he had to give up Petersburg, so our train went very slowly, not knowing what was ahead of us, and about two hours before daylight the train was stopped and we were ordered off and into line, and we marched about one mile and then we were in sight of Petersburg and it was all on fire. We were on the west side of the Appomatox river, and then we were notified Lee had vacated Petersburg and gone, and our officers received orders from a courier from General Lee for us to follow as fast as we could, so we started out on a road leading from Petersburg, and had gone about a mile to our left when there were two magazines about a quarter of a mile from each other, and one exploded about two or three minutes after the other and the concussion was so great that it almost jerked our line to their knees. It was terrific. We were on a forced march then until we caught up with our command. From then on there was fighting somewhere on our lines almost day and night. Our Longstreet corps was protecting Lee's rear, and when we got to a place called Rice Station, the enemy was pressing us so hard General Lee saw he could not get across the river unless we could hold this point, Rice Station. Longstreet ordered his picket lines doubled. I was the one detailed from our company and our orders were to hold our lines at all hazards. This was late in the evening.

"We held the enemy back until just before daylight. Our command had all crossed the river by this time. It was expected we would be captured, but the officer in command of us had been notified by a scout that everything had crossed over the river and it was expected we would be captured, so our officer notified us and said he was going to make an effort to get across the river and not be captured and for us to follow when we got through a body of woods and came to the road not far from the bridge across the river, we saw the bridge was on fire, and made a run to see if we could get across.

"The bridge was on fire at both ends, but there was space enough so we could get by single file and we found our cavalry in line at the foot of the hill, with their pickets in front, and before we got past their lines the enemy was firing on us. They found they could not cross there, but up the river, near Farmville, they put us in a pontoon bridge and got across the river.

"I got to my company about noon near Farmville, but before that I passed by where there were a great many wagons parked together, and on fire, burning up, but before I got to my company they issued rations to the men—one pint of flour and a very small piece of bacon, so my messmates had mine for me. About the middle of the afternoon the enemy began to advance from where they had crossed the river on their pontoons in Farmville. We were ordered into line of battle and went forward to meet the enemy and drove them back and held our position until 12 o'clock that night, and then we were ordered to follow the rest of the army, and up to this time there had been several commands of our army captured. The next morning we overtook the rest of the army. That was on April 8, and there was considerable fighting at different points all that day in front of us. Our command was bringing up and protecting the rear of our army.

"We kept moving all day and night until about 2 o'clock in the morning. This was on the morning of April 9. When day came it was found the enemy had got in front of our army, and when we began to advance the fighting began in front from near Appomatox Court House, and they began to press us in the rear. The fighting commenced with us. Our division [Fields'] was on the road leading to Appomatox and was halted and ordered right face into line of battle, and when we got a short distance from the road upon an incline, we halted, and across a ravine there was the enemy, about 500 yards from us, as far as you could see, right and left. During this time the fighting had ceased in front of us. At this time General Lee and General Grant had met to negotiate terms of surrender, and General Grant sent a courier with flags of truce through our lines for his men to halt and not press on us, and during this time Lee and Grant had agreed upon terms of surrender. In front we heard no salutes or cheering from the enemy, but in our rear they commenced to fire salutes and cheer when they heard Lee had surrendered. When Grant heard those salutes and cheers he sent another courier through our lines, with orders to cease firing salutes and cheering, for they had nothing to cheer over, as they had let a little handful of men hold them back from Richmond and Petersburg for nine days and nights.

"During this time we were ordered to stack arms, and the next morning we were ordered to fall in line and to take our arms and march to Appomatox Court House, about two miles, and then we were marched between two lines of the enemy and stacked our arms and marched off and left them. In every direction you could see nothing but bluecoats. It was said that Lee did not surrender but between nine and ten thousands of arms, and that Grant had somewhere near one hundred thousand men. General Grant had lost fully one half of his army before he got to Appomatox. On the evening of April 11, late in the afternoon, we members of Fields' division were paroled and left to get home the best we could, and it took me until the first of May to get home."

Surrendering with Laseter were the following men of Company H:

W. V. Armistead
William F. Baker
Thomas A. Batchelor
B. F. Blasingame
Cicero P. Blasingame
James D. Callaway
Franklin M. Echols

M. V. Edwards
Seaborn F. Fambrough
Isaac W. Forrester
James J. Garrett
W. J. Garrett
Charles L. Hayes
F. M. Hayes

J. M. Hester
John Holder
Daniel Noonan Hudson
James M. Kent
Robert J. Mann
William A. Mann
Robert A. Mayfield
Jesse H. Melton
J. J. Melton
William Mitcham
James W. Morrow
David R. Myers
Robert E. Myers
Jesse W. Partin

W. A. Partin
Francis M. Peters
Harrison Preston
John P. Reed
Logan Henry Sigman
J. H. Sluder
James M. Smith
Augustus R. Stark
J. T. Tuck
Francis M. Wiley
John D. Wiley
T. W. Wiley
Rufus J. Williams

# Appendix

### MUSTER ROLL
### COMPANY H, 11th REGIMENT
### GEORGIA VOLUNTEER INFANTRY
### ARMY NORTHERN VIRGINIA, C.S.A.
### WALTON COUNTY, GEORGIA
### ("WALTON INFANTRY")

Nunnally, Matthew Talbot—Captain, July 3, 1861. Killed at Gettysburg, Pa., July 2, 1863, in Devil's Den.

McDaniel, Henry D.—1st Lieutenant, July 3, 1861. Appointed Quartermaster, July 15, 1861; Captain & A.Q.M., Aug. 29, 1862; Major, Nov. 8, 1862. Wounded at Funkstown, Md., July 10, 1863. Captured at Hagerstown, Md., July 12, 1863. Released at Johnson's Island, O., July 25, 1865.

Burson, George S.—2d Lieutenant, July 3, 1861. Detailed Acting Adjutant. Killed at 2d Manassas, Va., Aug. 30, 1862.

Arnold, Eugenius C., Jr.—2d Lieutenant, July 3, 1861. Elected 1st Lieutenant, Nov. 17, 1862; Captain, July 17, 1863. Resigned, disability, Mar. 22, 1865. Elected Captain of a cavalry company in State service.

Nunnally, Josiah E.—1st Sergeant, July 3, 1861. Wounded in left leg at 2d Manassas, Va., Aug. 30, 1862. Discharged, disability. Leg amputated after the war.

Eckles, John T.—2d Sergeant, July 3, 1861. Discharged, disease disability, at Centreville, Va., Jan. 27, 1862. Enlisted as a private in Co. D, 2d Regt. Ga. Cavalry, May 1, 1862. Paroled at Augusta, Ga., May 20, 1865.

Easley, Richard S.—3d Sergeant, July 3, 1861. Promoted

APPENDIX 77

2d Sergeant, Jan. 27, 1862; 1st Sergeant, July 17, 1863. Killed at Deep Bottom, Va., Aug. 16, 1864.

Richardson, William J.—4th Sergeant, July 3, 1861. Appointed 3d Sergeant, Jan. 27, 1862; Ordnance Sergeant, Sept. 9, 1862. Elected Jr. 2d Lieutenant, July 17, 1863. Wounded. On wounded furlough Aug. 31, 1864. No later record.

Baker, W. F.—1st Corporal, transferred to the non-commissioned staff as Q.M. Sergeant.

Smith, A. H.—2d Corporal, July 3, 1861. Promoted 1st Corporal; 4th Sergeant, January 27, 1862. Died of disease at Richmond, Va., April 13, 1862.

Preston, Richard M.—3d Corporal, promoted to 1st Corporal, July 3, 1861. Appointed 4th Sergeant, Aug. 1862. Killed at Rappahannock, Va., Aug. 23, 1862.

Sheats, James N.—3d Corporal, July 3, 1861. Appointed Ordance Sergeant, Dec. 15, 1862. Received pay Jan. 7, 1865. No later record. Pension records show he left command on 30 days' furlough Dec. 1864, and was unable to reach command.

Blasingame, Cicero P.—4th Corporal, July 3, 1861. Appointed 4th Sergeant, August 23, 1862. Elected Jr. 2d Lieutenant, November 17, 1862; 2d Lieutenant, July 17, 1863; 1st Lieutenant, March 22, 1865. Surrendered, Appomattox, Va., April 9, 1865.

Richardson, William C.—Fifer, July 3, 1861. Transferred to Co. F., 16th Regt. Ga. Inf., in exchange for W. M. Still, December 6, 1862. Returned to Co. H., 11th Regt. Ga. Inf. Killed at Wilderness, Va., May 6, 1864.

Wood, Thomas G.—Drummer, July 3, 1861. Died of disease at Richmond, Va., December 13, 1861.

Allen, James C.—Private, July 3, 1861. Discharged, disability at Richmond, Va., November 20, 1861.

Allen, William E.—Private, July 3, 1861. Discharged, disability, at Culpeper, Va., August 10, 1861.

Armistead, Francis F.—Private, March 23, 1862. Killed at 2d Manassas, Va., August 30, 1862.

Armistead, Jesse M.—Private, July 3, 1861. Sent to General Hospital, February 13, 1862. Died of tuberculosis in Chimborazo Hospital #2, Richmond, Va., June 18, 1862.

Armistead, W. V.—Private, March 6, 1862. Surrendered, Appomattox, Va., April 9, 1865.

Arnold, John H.—Private, July 3, 1861. Killed at Gettysburg, Pa., July 3, 1863.

Atha, John M.—Private, March 23, 1862. Died of typhoid fever in Chimborazo Hospital #5, at Richmond, Va., July 7, 1862.

Atha, Joshua—Private, July 3, 1861. Wounded, date and place not given. On wounded furlough August 31, 1864. No later record.

Atha, Thomas—Private, July 3, 1861. Admitted to Chimborazo Hospital #5, at Richmond, Va., May 14, 1862. Killed at Gettysburg, Pa., July 2, 1863.

Baker, William F.—Private, July 3, 1861. Appointed Quartermaster Sergeant, July 12, 1861. Surrendered, Appomattox, Va., April 9, 1865.

Barefield, William S.—Private, July 3, 1861. Died of disease in Culpeper, Va., hospital, January 5, 1862.

Barton, David—Private, July 3, 1861. Wounded at Knoxville, Tenn., November 29, 1863. At home on wounded furlough August 31, 1864. No later record.

Batchelor, Thomas A.—Private, July 3, 1861. Wounded at 2d Manassas, Va., August 30, 1862; through elbow of left arm at Gettysburg, Pa., July 2, 1863. Surrendered Appomattox, Va., April 9, 1865. (Born in Georgia, December 22, 1843)

Baxley, James A.—Private, September 25, 1861. Wounded in the leg at the battle of Manassas, Aug 30, 1862; at home on furlough. Paroled at Augusta, Ga., May 20, 1865.

Baxley, J. C.—Private, April 21, 1864. Captured at Wilderness, Va., May 6, 1864. Died of pneumonia in Elmira, N. Y., January 29, 1865.

Baxley, William A.—Private, July 3, 1861. Wounded at 2d Manassas, Va., August 30, 1862. Killed at Funkstown, Md., July 10, 1863. (Born in Walton County, Ga.)

Bennett, Asa—Private, Sept. 25, 1861. Killed at 2d Manassas, Va., Aug. 30, 1862.

Bennett, Washington—Private, March 23, 1862. Killed at 2d Manassas, Va., August 30, 1862.

Black, Asbury C.—Private, July 3, 1861. Roll for Aug. 31, 1864, last on file, shows him absent without leave. No later record.

Blackwell, John C.—Private, July 3, 1861. Captured at Gettysburg, Pa., July 5, 1863. Paroled at Fort Delaware, Del. Feb. 10, 1865. Received at James River, Va. for exchange Feb. 15, 1865. No later record.

APPENDIX 79

Blankenship, Robert R.—Private, July 3, 1861. Wounded in thigh at Yorktown, Va., April 16, 1862. Retired May 4, 1864. Captured in Walton County, Ga., July 23, 1864. Paroled at Camp Chase, O., March 4, 1865. Received at James River, Va. for exchange March 12, 1865. No later record.

Blasingame, Alonzo H.—Private July 3, 1861. Appointed 3d Corporal September, 1862. Wounded at Gettysburg, Pa., July 3, 1863. Roll for Aug. 31, 1864, last on file, shows he was detached as Commissary Sergeant at Beauregard's Headquarters. No later record.

Blasingame, B. F.—Private, July 3, 1861. Surrendered, Appomattox, Va., April 9, 1865. (Born in Walton County, Ga. July 16, 1830. Died at Jersey, Ga. April 21, 1911.)

Boyce, John H.—Private, July 3, 1861. Discharged, disability, at Culpeper, Va., Sept. 28, 1861.

Boyce, Marion Y.—Private, July 3, 1861. Discharged at Yorktown, Va., April 30, 1862.

Briscoe, Egbert B.—Private, July 3, 1861. Discharged, furnished H. H. Melton as substitute, Jan. 27, 1862. Enlisted as a private in Co. D, 2d Regt. Ga. Cavalry, May 1, 1862. Roll for Dec. 31, 1864, last on file, shows him absent without leave since August 10th. No later record.

Broadax, Joel—Private. Conscript. Disabled with disease at Richmond, Va.

Broadnax, William Cosby Dawson—Private. Wounded in the battle of Malvern Hill, in the foot with a minie ball, July 1, 1862. Transferred to Company E.

Brown, Joseph T.—Private, July 3, 1861. Discharged, disability, at Culpeper, Va., Nov. 20, 1861. Enlisted as a private in Co. D, 2d Regt. Ga. Cavalry, May 1, 1862. Captured at Sevierville, Tenn. Jan. 27, 1864. Exchanged at Rock Island, Ill. March 2, 1865. No later record.

Browning, John B.—Private, January 27, 1862. Substitute for W. J. Ivey. Wounded and captured at Gettysburg, Pa., July 2, 1863. Transferred from West Buildings Hospital at Baltimore, Md., to City Point, Va., for exchange, November 17, 1863. Discharged, disability, March 13, 1865.

Buse, Morton Y.—Private, July 3, 1861. Wounded at Malvern Hill, Va., July 1, 1862. Roll for Aug. 31, 1864, last on file, shows him in General Hospital. No later record.

Butler, William H.—Private, July 3, 1861. Discharged, disability, at Culpeper, Va., August 10, 1861.

Callaway, James D.—Private, September 25, 1861. Appointed 3d Corporal, December 15, 1862. Surrendered, Appomattox, Va., April 9, 1865.

Callaway, Joseph—Private, July 3, 1861. Discharged, disease disability, at Richmond, Va., November 10, 1861.

Cason, Thomas—Private, July 3, 1861. Discharged, disease disability, at Culpeper, Va., September 23, 1861.

Clay, Henry C.—Private, July 3, 1861. Wounded at Rappahannock, Va., August 28, 1862; at Gettysburg, Pa., July 2, 1863, and captured there, July 5, 1863. Paroled at DeCamp General Hospital, David's Island, N. Y. Harbor, September, 1863. Exchanged at City Point, Va., September 8, 1863. On wounded furlough August 31, 1864. No later record.

Clay, R. H.—Private, March 4, 1862. Died of disease between Yorktown and Richmond, Va., May 5, 1862.

Cooper, Henry J.—Private, July 3, 1861. Wounded and disabled at 2d Manassas, Va., August 30, 1862. Retired to Invalid Corps, July 2, 1864. (Born in Georgia May 8, 1836.)

Cooper, William H.—Private, July 3, 1861. Discharged, disability, Nov. 10, 1861. Reenlisted March 23, 1862. Wounded at 2d Manassas, Va., August 30, 1862. Killed at Gettysburg, Pa., July 2, 1863 (head wound).

Dalton, Jesse—Private, March 23, 1862. Lost arm in accident, September 23, 1862. Discharged, disability, June 20, 1862.

Davis, Reuben H.—Private, July 3, 1861. Died of disease at Richmond, Virginia, October 9, 1861.

Dickinson, B. C.—Private, July 3, 1861. Appears without remark as to presence or absence on roll for August 31, 1864. Transferred to Signal Corps.

Dickinson, John S.—Private. Conscript. Discharged, disease disability at Richmond, Va., August 10, 1862.

Echols, Franklin M.—Private, September 25, 1861. Surrendered, Appomattox, Va., April 9, 1865.

Edwards, M. V.—Private, July 3, 1861. Surrendered Appomattox, Va., April 9, 1865.

Edwards, William T.—Private, September 25, 1861. Wounded at 2d Manassas, Va., August 30, 1862. Died of wounds September 18, 1862. Buried in Thornrose Cemetery at Staunton, Va.

APPENDIX

Everette, John—Private, March 23, 1862. Died of disease at Winchester, Va., October 27, 1862.

Everette, S. H. (or S. M.?)—Private, July 3, 1861. Died at Richmond, Va., June 10, 1864. Buried Richmond's Hollywood Cemetery.

Fambrough, Seaborn F.—Private, July 3, 1861. Surrendered, Appomattox, Va., April 9, 1865.

Forrester, Isaac W.—Private, July 3, 1861. Surrendered, Appomattox, Va., April 9, 1865.

Garrett, James J.—Private, July 3, 1861. Wounded at Malvern Hill, Va., July 1, 1862; near Holly Springs, Va., August 14, 1864. Surrendered, Appomattox, Va., April 9, 1865.

Garrett, John H.—Private, September 25, 1861. Died of disease in Chimborazo Hospital at Richmond, Va., April 13, 1862.

Garrett, William H. H.—Private, July 3, 1861. Wounded at Malvern Hill, Va., July 1, 1862. Died of wounds in Medical College Hospital at Richmond, Va., August 6, 1862.

Garrett, W. J.—Private, March 6, 1862. Appointed 4th Sergeant September 22, 1862; 3d Sergeant; Ordinance Sergeant. Surrendered, Appomattox, Va., April 9, 1865.

Gibbs, Coleman John—Private, July 3, 1861. Absent without leave, March 15, 1862. Discharged because of disability, July 18, 1862.

Gibbs, Cornelius M.—Private, July 3, 1861. Died of disease in General Hospital at Richmond, Va., December 3, 1861.

Griffin, John W.—Private, July 3, 1861. Killed at Malvern Hill, Va., July 1, 1862.

Guthrie, James B.—Private, July 3, 1861. Roll for August 31, 1864, last on file, shows him present. No later record.

Guthrie, Rufus E.—Private, March 6, 1862. Wounded in left leg, necessitating amputation, at 2d Manassas, Va., August 30, 1862. At home wounded close of war.

Hamilton, William C.—Private, July 3, 1861. Died of disease at Richmond, Va., October 7, 1862. Buried in Thornrose Cemetery at Staunton, Va.

Hattaway, Richard Thomas (or Hadaway)—Private, March 1862. Died of apoplexy in General Hospital #18, at Richmond, Va., May 2, 1862.

Hawk, J. W.—Private, March 23, 1862. Died of disease at Richmond, Va., May 10, 1862.

Hawk, Thornton H.—Private, Sept. 25, 1861. Killed at 2d Manassas, Va., August 30, 1862.

Hawk, T. A.—Private, March 23, 1862. Killed at 2d Manassas, Va., August 30, 1862.

Hayes, Charles L.—Private, July 3, 1861. Surrendered, Appomattox, Va., April 9, 1865.

Hayes, F. M.—Enlisted as a private in Co. H. 8th Regt. Ga. Inf., March 21, 1863. Transferred to Co. H, 11th Regt. Ga. Inf., August 1, 1864. Surrendered, Appomattox, Va., April 9, 1865.

Hayes, James J.—Private, February 6, 1864. Died of disease at Danville, Va., June 30, 1864.

Hayes, J. B.—Private, March 6, 1862. Died of disease at Richmond, Va., May 31, 1862.

Hayes, Leonard B.—Private, September 25, 1861. Appointed 3d Corporal. Wounded and captured at Knoxville, Tenn., November 29, 1863. Died of wounds in U. S. General Hospital #5 at Knoxville, Tenn., November 29, 1863. Buried in public cemetery there.

Herndon, Elisha M., Sr.—Enlisted as a private in Co., B, 3d Battn. Ga. State Troops, Oct. 30, 1861. Discharged April 8, 1862. Enlisted as a private in Co. H, 42d Regt. Ga. Inf., May 1862. Captured at Vicksburg, Miss., July 4, 1863, and paroled there, July 6, 1863. Transferred to Co. H, 11th Regt. Ga. Inf. in 1863. Killed near Petersburg, Va., July 28, 1864.

Hester, J. M.—Private, March 22, 1862. Surrendered, Appomattox, Va., April 9, 1865.

Hester, Seaborn G.—Private, September 25, 1861. Appointed 1st Corporal, August 23, 1862. Killed at Funkstown, Md., July 10, 1863.

Holder, John—Private, July 3, 1861. Surrendered, Appomattox, Va., April 9, 1865.

Hudson, Daniel Noonan—Private, March 2, 1862. Surrendered, Appomattox, Va., April 9, 1865.

Humphrey, Josiah—Private, September 25, 1861. Died of typhoid pneumonia at Richmond, Va., May 13, 1862.

Ivey, Warren J.—Private, September 25, 1861. Discharged, furnished John B. Browning as substitute, January 27, 1862. Appointed 2d Corporal of Co. D, 2d Regt. Ga. Cavalry, May 1, 1862; Sergeant; 1st Sergeant. Roll for Dec. 31, 1864, last on file, shows him present.

APPENDIX

Ivey, Wilson L.–Private, July 3, 1861. Killed at 2d Manassas, Va., August 30, 1862.

Kent, Francis Samuel–Private, January, 1864. Pension records show he was at home sick, December 31, 1864, to close of war.

Kent, James M.–Private, October 4, 1864. Surrendered, Appomattox, Va., April 9, 1865. (Born in Walton County, Ga., August 4, 1847.)

Laseter, William Thomas–Private, March 6, 1862. Wounded at Wilderness, Va., May 6, 1864. Surrendered, Appomattox, Va., April 9, 1865.

Lowe, William L.–Private, March 6, 1862. Died of disease at Richmond, Va., July 10, 1862.

Malcom, James D.–Private, September 25, 1861. Wounded in arm, necessitating amputation, at Suffolk, Va., May 15, 1863. On wounded furlough close of war.

Malcom, John Thomas–Private, March 6, 1862. Wounded at Sharpsburg, Md., September 17, 1862. In Division Hospital, August 31, 1864. No later record.

Mann, James A.–See private, Co. E.

Mann, Robert J.–Private, July 3, 1861. Appointed 2d Corporal. Surrendered, Appomattox, Va., April 9, 1865. (Born in Georgia.)

Mann, William A.–Private, July 3, 1861. Wounded at 2nd Manassas, Va., August 30, 1862. Surrendered, Appomattox, Va., April 9, 1865.

Maughon, Francis M.–Private, March 23, 1862. Discharged, disability, at Richmond, Va., Nov. 16, 1862. Enlisted as a private in Co. G, 42d Regt. Ga. Inf., Sept. 23, 1863. Appears on roll of Second Georgia Hospital at Augusta, Ga. dated Oct. 31, 1864, as present. Roll dated Feb. 28, 1865, shows him on furlough at home in Walton County, Ga.

Maughon, James R.–See private, Co. E.

Mayfield, Robert A.–Private, September 25, 1861. Surrendered, Appomattox, Va., April 9, 1865.

McMahan, Pleasant L.–See private, Co. E.

Melton, A. A.–Private, July 5, 1862. On detail duty at Lynchburg, Va., Aug. 31, 1864. No later record.

Melton, Barnett M.–Enlisted, as a private in Co. A, 10th Regt. Alabama Inf., June 4, 1861. Transferred to Co. H, 11th Regt. Ga. Inf., Nov. 18, 1861. Wounded at Deep Bottom, Va.,

August 16, 1864. Died of wounds in an ambulance on way to city, August 17, 1864.

Melton, B. W.—Private, March 6, 1862. Wounded in arm, necessitating amputation, at Deep Bottom, Va., August 16, 1864. Retired to Invalid Corps, March 22, 1865.

Melton, D. E.—Private, August 26, 1862. Wounded at Furlow's Mill, Va., November 13, 1863. On detail duty as nurse in Augusta, Ga. hospital, August, 1864. No later record.

Melton, Harris H.—Private, January 21, 1862. Substitute for E. B. Briscoe. Prisoner of war in Gettysburg, Pa., hospital, July 2, 1863.

Melton, Jesse H.—Private, July 3, 1861. Surrendered, Appomattox, Va., April 9, 1865.

Melton, J. J.—Private, February 6, 1864. Surrendered, Appomattox, Va., April 9, 1865.

Melton, William T.—Private, July 3, 1861. Killed at Knoxville, Tenn., November 11, 1863.

Mitcham, William—Private, July 3, 1861. Wounded at 2d Manassas, Va., August 30, 1862. Appointed 4th Corporal. Surrendered, Appomattox, Va., April 9, 1865.

Moon, Marmon B.—Private, July 3, 1861. Wounded in 1862. Sent to General Hospital, March 8, 1862. Discharged, disability, at Richmond, Va., August 10, 1862.

Morrow, James W.—Private, July 3, 1861. Appointed 4th Sergeant, April 13, 1862; Ordnance Sergeant, August 1862. Elected 2d Lieutenant, Sept. 9, 1862; 1st Lieutenant, July 17, 1863; Captain, March 22, 1865, Surrendered, Appomattox, Va., April 9, 1865.

Myers, David R.—Private, July 3, 1861. Appointed Corporal, Sept. 1862; 1st Sergeant, Aug. 30, 1864. Surrendered, Appomattox, Va., April 9, 1865.

Myers, Robert E.—Private, July 3, 1861. Surrendered, Appomattox, Va., April 9, 1865.

Myers, R. W. (or P. W.)—Private, March 23, 1862. Killed at 2d Manassas, Va., August 30, 1862.

Needham, Charles—Private, July 3, 1861. Died of disease at Culpeper, Va., September 14, 1861.

Needham, Rolly—Private, July 3, 1861. Wounded at 2d Manassas, Va., August 30, 1862. Discharged, disability, July 4, 1864.

Odom, James W.—Private, July 3, 1861. Wounded in left

APPENDIX 85

arm, necessitating amputation, at camp near Manassas, Va., July 1861. Discharged, disability, at Richmond, Va., August 6, 1861.

Partin, Benjamin—Private, February 6, 1864. Died of disease, August 12, 1864.

Partin, Berry W.—Private, March 23, 1862. Discharged, disability, at Richmond, Va. in 1862.

Partin, Jesse W.—Private, August 10, 1862. Surrendered, Appomattox, Va., April 9, 1865.

Partin, J. J.—Private, March 23, 1862. Admitted to Chimborazo Hospital #2, at Richmond, Va., May 14, 1862. Transferred to Danville, Va., June 28, 1862. Died of measles, July 1, 1862.

Partin, William M.—Private, March 23, 1862. Killed at Gettysburg, Pa., July 2, 1863.

Partin, W. A.—Private, March 6, 1862. Surrendered, Appomattox, Va., April 9, 1865.

Peters, A. F.—Private, March 6, 1862. Captured at Knoxville, Tenn., December 3, 1863. Paroled at Rock Island, Ill., February 25, 1865. Received at James River, Va., for exchange, March 5, 1865. No later record.

Peters, Francis M.—Private, Sept. 25, 1861. Wounded at Gettysburg, Pa., July 2, 1863. Surrendered, Appomattox, Va., April 9, 1865.

Peters, James F. (or James T.)—Private, March 23, 1862. Died of disease at Richmond, Va., May 20, 1862.

Peters, J. W.—Private, March 9, 1863. Roll for August 31, 1864, last on file, shows him present. No later record.

Preston, Harrison, H. G.—Private, July 3, 1861. Appointed Corporal. Wounded at 2d Manassas, Va., August 30, 1862. Appointed 3d Sergeant, September 9, 1862. Surrendered, Appomattox, Va., April 9, 1865.

Prince, Epps—Private, March 11, 1863. Under sentence of Court Martial at Richmond, Va., August 31, 1864. No later record.

Ramey, George W.—Private, May 13, 1862. Discharged, disability, at Richmond, Va., August 1, 1862.

Reed, John P.—Private, July 3, 1861. Surrendered, Appomattox, Va., April 9, 1865.

Reaves, Thompson (or Reeves)—Private, July 3, 1861. Discharged, disability, Dec. 17, 1861. Promoted hospital steward. Enlisted as a private in Co. D, 2d Regt. Ga. Cavalry, May 1, 1862. Appears only on roll for May-June, 1862.

Richardson, James J.—Private, July 3, 1861. Discharged, disability, at Centreville, Va., December 24, 1861.

Roberts, Isaac M.—See private, Co. E.

Robertson, Theophilus L.—Private, September 25, 1861. Died at Richmond, Va., May 15, 1862.

Shellnut, Henry H.—Private, July 3, 1861. Died of disease near Williamsburg, Va., May 5, 1862.

Sigman, Gus P.—Private, Feb. 6, 1864. On sick furlough, August 31, 1864. No later record. (Born in Ga. Died in Atlanta, Ga., June 12, 1925.)

Sigman, Logan Henry—Private, July 3, 1861. Surrendered, Appomattox, Va., April 9, 1865.

Sitton, H. C.—Private. (See letters on file at Ga. State Dept. of Archives, Atlanta, Georgia.)

Sluder, Augustus L.—Private, July 3, 1861. Wounded in leg, necessitating amputation, at Gettysburg, Pa., July 2, 1863. On wounded furlough close of war.

Sluder, J. H.—Private, April 13, 1864. Surrendered, Appomattox, Va., April 9, 1865.

Sluder, William D.—Private, July 3, 1861. Wounded at Fredericksburg, Va., December 13, 1862. Captured at Social Circle, Ga., July 23, 1864. Sent to Camp Chase, O., August 10, 1864. where he was released on taking oath of allegiance to U. S. Govt., December 13, 1864.

Smith, Calvin L.—Private, July 3, 1861. Discharged, disability, at Richmond, Va., November 10, 1861. Enlisted as a private in Co. D., 2d Regt. Ga. Cavalry,. May 1, 1862. Captured at Wills Valley, Alabama, February 1, 1864. Released at Rock Island, Ill., June 21, 1865.

Smith, Elijah—Private, March 6, 1862. Wounded at Gettysburg, Pa., July 2, 1863. Died of wounds, August 1863.

Smith, E. A.—Private, March 23, 1862. Wounded at 2d Manassas, Va., August 30, 1862. Paid at Orange Court House, Va., May 17, 1863. No later record.

Smith, James M.—Private, March 6, 1862. Wounded at Gettysburg, Pa., July 2, 1863. Surrendered, Appomattox, Va., April 9, 1865.

APPENDIX 87

Smith, Joel—Private, July 3, 1861. Wounded, date and place not given. On wounded furlough, August 31, 1864. No later record.

Smith, John B.—Private, September 25, 1861. Discharged, disability, at Richmond, Va., November 10, 1861.

Smith, John H.—Private, March 6, 1862. Wounded at Gettysburg, Pa., July 2, 1863. On wounded furlough, August 31, 1864. No later record.

Smith, Miles—Private, July 3, 1861. Wounded, date and place not given. In hospital, wounded, August 31, 1864. No later record.

Smith, W. H.—Private, March 6, 1862. Wounded at Funkstown, Md., July 10, 1863. On wounded furlough, August 31, 1864. No later record.

Stark, Augustus R.—Private, July 3, 1861. Surrendered, Appomattox, Va., April 9, 1865.

Still, William Martin—Enlisted as a private in Co. F, 16th Regt. Ga. Inf., July 19, 1861. Admitted to Chimborazo Hospital #5, at Richmond, Va., in 1862. Returned to duty, Sept. 18, 1862. Transferred to Co. H, 11th Regt, Ga. Inf., in exchange for W. C. Richardson, Dec. 6, 1862. Admitted to General Hospital #9, at Richmond, Va., July 26, 1863; transferred to General Hospital #21, there July 27, 1863, and died of bronchitis, September 6, 1863.

Thomasson, Henry C.—Private, July 3, 1861. Wounded in arm, necessitating amputation, and captured at Gettysburg, Pa., July 2, 1863. Exchanged at David's Island, N. Y. Harbor, January 1864. On detail duty as Provost Guard at Ga. Railroad in 1864, to close of war. Paroled at Augusta, Ga., May 6, 1865.

Thompson, James T.—Private, July 3, 1861. In Ga. Hospital #2, Richmond, Va., October 30th, 1861. At Camp Sam Jones in January, February, and March, 1862; Camp near Corning Court House on March 26, 1862; Camp Winder, Richmond, Va., April 12, 1862; New Kent County, Va., May 13, 1862; Richmond, June 20, 1862, 2½ miles east of Richmond, July 15, 1862; Winchester, Virginia, September 22, 1862; near Winchester, Virginia, October 1, 1862, and October 5, 1862 (his last letter home); died of smallpox at Winchester, Va., November 1, 1862.

Thompson, John W.—Private, March 6, 1862. Wounded in

right thigh and permanently disabled, at 2d Manassas, Va., August 30, 1862. Retired to Invalid Corps, July 2, 1864. Pension records show he enlisted in Captain Arnold's Co. Ga. Militia, November 1864. Surrendered Macon, Ga., April, 1865. (Born in Georgia, January 30, 1844. Died in Walton County, Ga., November 18, 1919).

Thompson, Joseph R.—Private, July 3, 1861. Died of disease in Orange Court House, Va., hospital April 5, 1862.

Tillman, James W.—Private, July 3, 1861. Discharged, furnished substitute, November 10, 1862.

Toler, Benjamin J.—Private, July 3, 1861. Discharged, disability, at Richmond, Va., November 10, 1861. Reenlisted March 23, 1862. No later record.

Tuck, G. W.—Private, March 23, 1862. Died of disease in Richmond, Va., June 5, 1862.

Tuck, Josiah L.—Private, July 3, 1861. Killed at 2d Manassas, Va., August 30, 1862.

Tuck, J. T.—Private, July 3, 1861. Wounded at 2d Manassas, Va., August 30, 1862; Knoxville, Tenn., November 29, 1863. Surrendered, Appomattox, Va., April 9, 1865.

Tuck, Seaborn G.—Private, September 25, 1861. Wounded at 2d Manassas, Va., August 30, 1862. Appointed Ensign, June 17, 1864. Elected 1st Lieutenant. Paroled in Virginia in 1865.

Watson, Bennett—Private, May 13, 1862. Lost arm in accident. Absent, August, 1864.

Watson, S. P.—Private, July 3, 1861. Killed at Knoxville, Tenn., November 29, 1863.

Whittle, Joseph L.—See private, Co. E.

Wiley, Francis M.—Private, July 3, 1861. Surrendered, Appomattox, Va., April 9, 1865.

Wiley, Isaac H.—Private, September 9, 1862. Died of hemorrhage of the lungs at Camp Lee Hospital, Richmond, Va., January 14, 1863.

Wiley, James M.—Appointed 2d Sergeant of Co. B, 1st Regt. Ga. Inf. (Ramsey's), March 18, 1861. Discharged, disability, August 18, 1861. Enlisted as a private in Co. H, 11th Regt. Ga. Inf., September 25, 1861. Wounded at Wilderness, Va., May 6, 1864. On wounded furlough, August 31, 1864. No later record.

Wiley, John D.—Private, July 3, 1861. Appointed Corporal,

APPENDIX 89

September, 1862; 2d Sergeant, June 1, 1864. Surrendered, Appomattox, Va., April 9, 1865.

Wiley, T. W.—Private, July 3, 1861. Surrendered, Appomattox, Va., April 9, 1865.

Wiley, William J.—Private, September 25, 1861. Wounded at Gettysburg, Pa., July 2, 1863, and captured in hospital there, July 1863. Sent to General Hospital at York, Pa., November 15, 1863, where he died from gunshot wound in lung, January 2, 1864. Buried from hospital, January 3, 1864.

Williams, Augustus E.—Enlisted as a private in Co. H, 8th Regt. Louisiana Inf., June 8, 1861. Transferred to Co. H, 11th Regt. Ga. Inf., March 12, 1863. Appointed 2d Sergeant, July 17, 1863. Killed at Cold Harbor, Va., June 2, 1864.

Williams, Lucillus A.—Private, July 3, 1861. Appointed Corporal, January 1, 1862. Killed at 2d Manassas, Va., August 30, 1862.

Williams, Rufus J.—Private, July 3, 1861. Detailed Musician. Surrendered, Appomattox, Va., April 9, 1865.

Witcofskey, William—Private, July 3, 1861. Discharged, disability, May 16, 1862.

Woodruff, Clifford H.—Private, July 3, 1861. Killed at Gettysburg, Pa., July 2, 1863.

Woodruff, John W.—Private, August 7, 1862. Left arm disabled at Fredericksburg, Va., December 13, 1862. Admitted to General Hospital at Petersburg, Va., June 24, 1864, and transferred to Richmond, Va., same date. Roll for August 31, 1864, last on file, shows him absent. No later record.

# Notes

## INTRODUCTION

1. Matthew Talbot Nunnally letter to Molly and Mark (his sister Mary and her husband), dated Jan. 16, 1862, which is part of the Sullivan private papers. Used by permission of Mrs. Martha F. Sullivan, Savannah, Georgia. (Captain Nunnally was born in Walton County, Georgia, March 18, 1839, the son of William Branch and Mary Talbot Nunnally.)

2. Kittrell J. Warren, *History of the 11th Regiment Georgia Volunteers* (1863). Hereafter cited as Warren. See also Kittrell J. Warren, *Life and Public Service of an Army Straggler* (Athens: University of Georgia Press, 1961, ed. by Floyd Watkins), for further information regarding Warren's private life.

## CHAPTER I

1. James G. Randall, *Civil War and Reconstruction* (Boston: D. C. Heath Co., 1955), pp. 274-277. For fuller account of battle see Robert M. Johnston, *Bull Run: Its Strategy and Tactics* (Boston: Houghton Mifflin, 1913); Clement Eaton, *A History of the Southern Confederacy* (New York: The Macmillan Company, 1954), pp. 152-154. Hereafter cited as Eaton.

2. Eaton, p. 152.

3. *Ibid.*

4. At Winchester, Col. Thomas Jackson received a letter from General Robert E. Lee dated July 3, 1861, notifying him that he had been appointed Brigadier-General. This appointment meant that Jackson would not be separated from his beloved brigade, which he had commanded as Colonel under General Joseph E. Johnston. Frank E. Vandiver, *Mighty Stonewall* (New York: McGraw-Hill, 1957), pp. 155-169. Hereafter cited as Vandiver. Douglas Southall Freeman, *Lee's Lieutenants* (New York: Charles Scribner's Sons, 1942), pp. 45-61. Hereafter cited as Freeman.

5. Warren, pp. 28-29.

6. Robert L. Dabney, *Life & Campaigns of Lt. Gen. Thos. J. Jackson (Stonewall Jackson)* (New York: Blelock and Company, 1866), p. 213.

7. Early muster rolls of Company H indicate that the regiment was mustered into service July 3 in Atlanta, Ga., by Major Calhoun and arrived at Richmond, Va., July 10. They left Richmond via North Railroad for Winchester on July 15 and arrived on the 18th. Marched from Winchester July 19 and reached Manassas July 22 and camped near battle ground until August 1, when they moved to Camp Bartow, For published letters of James Thomas Thompson, see July 1962 issue of *The Virginia*

NOTES

*Magazine of History and Biography*, Vol. 70, No. 3, letter of July 23, 1861, p. 315, ed. by Aurelia Austin. Hereafter cited as Austin, *Va. Mag.*

8. Probably Thompson's cousin. The Easleys were half brothers of Thomas Thompson, young James's father.

9. It was necessary for Thompson to travel 25 miles to Atlanta, approximately 300 miles to Savannah, unless he went by Augusta, and then to Virginia, which accounts for most of this high mileage. For Thompson's letter of July 27, 1861, in its entirety, see Austin, *Va. Mag.* pp. 315-316.

10. Henry Kyd Douglas, *I Rode With Stonewall* (Chapel Hill: University of North Carolina Press, 1940), p. 10. Hereafter cited as Douglas.

11. Eaton, pp. 153-154.

12. Official records reveal that approximately 500 Union men were killed and the Confederate dead were reported as being 378. See Eaton, p. 154.

13. Vandiver, pp. 166-167.

14. Eaton, p. 125.

CHAPTER II

1. Sullivan papers, Nunnally letter, Jan. 16. 1862.

2. Mary Jane Thompson, oldest daughter of Thomas Thompson, said her father was extremely honest in his declarations to the tax collector, and perhaps one reason why his tax bill was higher than his neighbors' bills was because he insisted on declaring every plow share and piece of farm equipment, regardless of its age. However, Thomas Thompson owned land in DeKalb, Gwinnett, and Fulton counties. Aurelia Austin, *Austin-Ayers, Wells-Thompson, and Allied Families*, unpublished. Hereafter cited as Austin, Family History.

3. One plot being that of the present location of the Fulton Bag and Cotton Mill. Austin, Family History.

4. *Ibid*. In later life Thomas Thompson and his wife, Lucinda Hardman Thompson, joined Antioch Congregational Church. Mary Jane and her sisters joined Mt. Cavalry Methodist Church. After her marriage to James Wells, Mary Jane joined the Stone Mountain Baptist Church, Stone Mountain, Ga. Later she and her husband transferred to the Tucker Baptist Church, which James A. Wells helped organize.

5. Eaton, p. 101.

6. Comment on muster roll of Company H states that the company moved to Camp Bartow after August 1. Vandiver, p. 167, states that Jackson decided to move his men because the water was bad and the location depressing. On August 2 they began moving to a site near Centreville on the road to Fairfax Courthouse.

7. Austin, *Va. Mag.*, pp. 316-317.

8. Warren, p. 29.

9. Vandiver, p. 167, states that Quartermaster Harman found this campsite and persuaded farmer Utterbach to permit its use by the soldiers. The camp was named for Major Harman.

10. Record of Events, Company H for Sept. 1861, Georgia State Department of Archives and History, Atlanta.

11. Sullivan Papers, Nunnally letter, Jan. 16, 1862.

12. Warren, p. 29.

13. *Ibid*, p. 30.

14. Austin, *Va. Mag.*, pp. 317-318.

15. Messenger was Thomas Thompson's fine breeding horse.

16. Austin, *Va. Mag.*, p. 318.

CHAPTER III

1. Approximately 40% of the Tarheels could not read or write. Many signed their muster rolls with

an X. This is higher than the percentage for the Southern army as a whole. Eaton, p. 101.

2. Austin, *Va. Mag.*, p. 319. Record of events covering period July 3-Dec. 31, 1861, showed that Company H did picket duty on the Frying Pan Road the 5th and 20th of November and also on the 5th and 20th of December 1861. "Nothing worthy of note occuring." See microfilm in Georgia State Department of Archives and History, Atlanta.

3. Sullivan papers, Nunnally letter, Jan. 16, 1862.

4. Warren, p. 31.

5. Sullivan papers, Nunnally letter, Jan. 16, 1862.

6. Austin, *Va. Mag.*, p. 320.

7. Henry Dickerson McDaniel (1836-1926) was a graduate of Atlanta high schools, and studied law in Atlanta. He held an A.B. degree from Mercer University, graduating with the highest honors of the class of 1856. He began the practice of law in Walton County in 1857. He was elected as Walton County's delegate to the State Convention of 1861 and was its youngest member.

McDaniel opposed secession, but finally signed the secession ordinance. He joined the Walton Infantry; participated in the campaigns in Virginia, Pennsylvania, and Maryland; was promoted Major; was severely wounded near Funkstown, Maryland; was captured as a prisoner of war after which he spent five months in hospitals, then was confined to a Federal prison at Johnson's Island, Ohio; released July, 1865.

On returning to Monroe, Georgia (Walton County), he resumed the practice of law; was elected to the State Legislature in 1872; was elected senator in 1874 and served his state in this capacity for eight years. He assumed the office of Governor of Georgia in 1884 upon the death of Governor Alexander H. Stephens and was thereafter elected for a term of four years. At the expiration of his governorship he returned to private law practice in Monroe. He served as a Trustee of the University of Georgia in 1884 and was President of the Board of Trustees in 1889. In 1907 the University of Georgia gave him an honorary L.L.D. degree. He was a Baptist, an active churchman, and served as Trustee of the Southern Theological Seminary at Louisville, Kentucky, from 1883-90. He married the former Hester Caroline Felker in December, 1865, and they had two children, Sanders and Gipsy. He died in 1926. From a short biographical sketch furnished by Gov. McDaniels' grandson, Henry Tichenor of Monroe.

8. Austin, *Va. Mag.*, pp. 320-321.

9. Richard Mason, *The Gentleman's Pocket Farrier . . . with a Supplement . . . by J. S. Skinner.* A famous book of which there are many editions.

10. Austin, unpublished letters of James Thomas Thompson, private collection of the editor.

11. *Ibid.*

12. It was imperative that the Confederacy preserve the lives of its horses. A shortage of horses occurred in the South in the summer of 1862. The mortality rate of army horses was high, the average life of a horse being seven and one-half months in the artillery and transportation services. In the cavalry the life expectancy was even shorter. Eaton, p. 104.

13. Bob was one of two male slaves owned by Thomas Thompson. Austin, Family History.

14. Austin, *Va. Mag.*, pp. 321-322.

15. Warren, p. 32.

16. Austin, *Va. Mag.*, p. 322.

17. *Ibid*, pp. 323-324.

18. Sullivan papers, Nunnally letter, Jan. 16, 1862.

# NOTES

19. Eaton, p. 165.
20. Austin, *Va. Mag.*, p. 324.

## CHAPTER IV

1. Bruce Catton, *The Army of the Potomac* (New York: Doubleday, 1951), p. 107. Hereafter cited as Catton, *Army of Potomac*.
2. Eaton, pp. 165-166; Sanger, D. B. and T. R. Hay, *James Longstreet* (Baton Rouge: Louisiana State University Press, 1952), pp. 38-49. Hereafter cited as Sanger-Hay.
3. Laseter, William T., *Shreveport Journal*, Oct. 31, 1929. A Large portion of Laseter's article is reproduced in the final chapter. Hereafter cited as Laseter article.
4. Warren, p. 35.
5. Sullivan papers, Nunnally letter, Jan. 16, 1862.
6. *Ibid.*
7. Austin, *Va. Mag.*, pp. 324-325.
8. Warren, p. 36.
9. Eaton, pp. 166-67; Sanger-Hay, pp. 56-58
10. Eaton, pp. 166-67; Sanger-Hay, pp. 62-76.
11. Eaton, p. 167.
12. Warren, p. 36.
13. Austin, *Va. Mag.*, pp. 325-326.
14. Eaton, p. 169; Sanger-Hay, pp. 70-71.
15. Austin, *Va. Mag.*, p. 327.

## CHAPTER V

1. Historians have referred to this as "Lee's great tactical blunder." Douglas Southall Freeman puts part of the blame for this failure on Lee's subordinates, particularly Nuger, Magruder, and Jackson, because of their poor handling of artillery, bad staff work, etc., which prevented Lee being in close touch with various units of his army. Eaton, pp. 169-170; Sanger-Hay, pp. 73-76.
2. Sullivan papers, Nunnally letter, Jan. 16, 1862.
3. Austin, *Va. Mag.*, p. 328.
4. Eaton, p. 171.
5. Warren, p. 45.
6. Warren, p. 45.
7. Austin, *Va. Mag.*, pp. 328-329.
8. Eaton, p. 191.
9. See Nunnally's comments on next page. Also Eaton, p. 191.
10. Sullivan papers, Nunnally letter, Jan. 16, 1862.
11. Austin, *Va. Mag.*, pp. 329-30.

## CHAPTER VI

1. Vandiver, p. 202, 266.
2. Austin, *Va. Mag.*, pp. 330-331.
3. Sullivan papers, Nunnally letter, Jan. 16, 1862.
4. *Ibid.*
5. *Ibid.*

## CHAPTER VII

1. Laseter article.
2. Sanger-Hay, p. 140.
3. *Ibid.*, p. 147.
4. Laseter article.
5. Sanger-Hay, p. 151.
6. *Ibid.*, p. 155.
7. Laseter article; Sanger-Hay, pp. 156-172, 173-188.
8. Eaton, p. 203.
9. Sanger-Hay, pp. 189-199; Laseter article.
10. Sanger-Hay, p. 193.
11. *Ibid.*

# Index

☆ ☆ ☆ ☆ ☆ ☆ ☆ ☆ ☆ ☆

Alexander, E. P., warned Confederates of enemy approach, 6
Alexandria, railroad, 2, 12; road, 14, 45; town, 2
Anderson, Brig. Gen. George Thomas (Tige), 11th Ga., ix, 5, 20, 25; Dam #1, 33; at Manassas, 44, 45, 46; near Richmond, 40, New Kent County, Va., 35, 36; Pickett's charge, 64
Appomattox, court house, xii; river, 72; surrender, 73
Army of Potomac, at Camp Sam Jones, 23
Army of Shenandoah, under Joe Johnston, evacuated Winchester, 3
Arnold, Eugenius C., Jr., Second Lt., 11th Ga., ix, 21, 39
Arnold, John H., killed at Gettysburg, 64
Artillery, 1, 7, 14, 17, 31, 32, 33, 43, 50, 52, 53, 57, 63, 69

Barclay, Dr. John, 41
Barrett, Dr. William S., on duty Ga. Hospital, 19
Bartow, Col. Francis S., at Manassas, 3, 6
Beauregard, Gen. Pierre G. T., at Manassas, x, 2, 3, 4, 5; meeting with Jefferson Davis, 7
Beaver Dam Creek, battle of, 39
Bee, Brig. Gen. Barnard E., names Stonewall Jackson, 6
Blackburn's Ford, Longstreet guarding, 5
Blackwater, Longstreet to start for, 60

Blankets, Confederates' use of, xi, 3, 26, 27, 30, 33, 34, 57
Blasingame, Cicero P., Fourth Corp., 11th Ga. Volunteers, ix
Blue Ridge Mountains, 11th Ga. crossing, x, 2, 59; Longstreet covering gaps, 62
Boonsboro (South Mountain, battle of), Crampton Gap, 50
Box Cars, 2, 6, 25, 29, 72
Braddock Road, Confederate camp, 14
Brown, Governor Joseph E., Soldiers' complaint about blankets, 30
Buckeyton, on march to Frederick, Md., 46
Bull Run (see also Manassas), battles, 1, 2, 5, 7, 44, 47, 54
Bull's Gap (near Greenville, Tenn.), 68
Burnside, Gen. Ambrose, at Knoxville, 68
Burson, George S., Second Lt., 11th Ga. ix; shoes, 55

Camp Bartow, 11, 12, 13
Camp Centerville, 20, 22
Camp Sam Jones, 23, 25
Camp Winder, 29, 30
Carroll, Tom, 40
Centreville, meeting of generals with Jeff Davis, 7; massing around, 15, 16, 17, 19; railroad, 25; Confederate camp, 27; Union Army at, 28
Chambersburg, Pa., and Ewell, 62
Chancellorsville, Va., Gen. Lee at, 61; Jackson fatally wounded at, 62

# INDEX

Charleston, S. C., Confederates donate to sufferers, 22
Chickahominy River, Confederates march along, 34; picket duty, 36; Federals south of, 38
City Point, artillery on James River nearby, 43
Clay, John (or Jim), expected in camp, 41
Clothing, xi, 3, 8, 14, 23, 24, 26, 28, 29, 33, 40, 46, 55, 56
Cobb, Gen. Howell, 11th under command, 35; issued food, 36; enemy attack on mountainside, 55
Cochran, Havel, 5
Cochran, Seaborn, 38
Colley, R. (Walton County), 12
Colors, 57, 71
Colwell, Seele, 5; DeKalb Co. man hospitalized, 5
Commissary stores, x
Company H, 59, 71
Confederates, 2, 5, 6, 7, 10, 31, 33, 35, 37, 39, 44, 47
Congress, 1, 18
Corning County, Va., Confederate camp, 28
Culpeper, Va., troops marched to, 27; layover at, 29; Gen. Pope at, 47; Longstreet occupied, 67

Dabney, Dr. R. L., explains 11th Ga. delay at Bull Run, 4
Dams 1, 2, and 3 (Confederate breast works), 32; Dam 1 occupied by 11th Ga., 34
Darby Town Road, Confederates occupied below Richmond, 71
Davis, Jefferson, meets generals at Centreville, 7; reported in Norfolk, 30
DeKalb troops, camped near Thompson, 5
Devil's Den, death place of Capt. Nunnally, 11th Ga. Infantry, 63

Easley, Benjamin, visiting son in First Ga. hospital, 17, 26
Easley, Richard S., Third Sgt., 11th Ga., ix; ill, 10, 26; killed Deep Bottom, Va., 70
Eckles, John T., Second Sgt., 11th Ga., ix

Eighth Georgia Regiment, ix, x, 2, 4, 6, 32, 35, 36, 44, 63, 69
England, Confederates hoped for support, 62
Evans, Major Nathan, 11th Ga. under, 6, 16
Ewell, marching toward Wrightsville, 62; Culpeper, Va., 63

Fairfax, Confederate troops left, 17
Fairfax Court House, Confederate camp 13, 14, moved from, 16
Falls Church, Confederates marched to, 13; picket duty, 14
Farmville, Va., 11th Georgia at, 73
Federal Navy, McClellan has protection of, 39
Field's Division, loaded on flat cars for Petersburg, 72
Flags (see also colors), Grant's flags of truce, 74
Food, good, 3, 8, 18, 20, 21, 22, 24, 25, 33, 36, 40, 45, 48, 52, 58; bad, 33, 34; 50; lack of, 33, 73
Fort Donelson, Tenn., 25
Fort Monroe, Va., McClellan at 29, 31
Fort Sumpter, S. C., first shots of war, 24
Fowler, Capt. (DeKalb County), 5
France, and Napoleon III, 62
Frederick, Md., confederates at, 46, 47
Fredericksburg, Va., march to, 29; battle, 30, 59; Gen. Hill at, 63; plank road to, 68
Freeman, Douglas Southall, 64
Fremantle, Lt. Col. James Arthur Lyon (Coldsteam Guards, England), 65
French, Gen. Wm. H., Lee needs help of, 61

Gaines's Mill, 39
Games, 22
Georgia, 1, 22, 23, 25, 26
Georgians, 35
Germantown, Va., 15
Gettysburg, Pa., 62, 63, 64, 65
Glendale (Frayser's Farm), 39
Gordonsville, Va., 2
Grant, Gen. U. S., at surrender, 74
Guerrilla shooting, 34

Gunboats, 35, 43, 70
Guns (see artillery), 7

Hagerstown, Pa., Ewell through to Pa., 62; supplies for men, 66
Hamilton, Doctor (Stone Mountain, Ga.), 44
Hampton, Wade, S. C. Aristocrats, 6
Hardman, Elizabeth (Halifax Co., Virginia), 10
Hardman, Ewell, 40
Hardman, John, Jr. (Lexington, Ga. and DeKalb Co., Ga.), 9, 41
Hardman, John, Sr. (Halifax Co., Va.), 10
Hardman, Mary Cochran, 9
Hardman, Susan, 40
Hardman, Uriah, 40
Harper's Ferry, Stonewall Jackson at, 50; Meade moved via, 67
Harrisburg, Pa., Longstreet at, 62
Heintzelman, Gen., fooled by McGruder's "Quaker" guns, 32
Henry House Hill, Gen. B. E. Bee killed here, 6
Henry, Mrs. Judith (owner of Henry House), 6
Hester, Seaborn (Sebe), killed at Funkstown, Md., 66, 82
Hill, A. P., attacked Federals at Mechanicsville, 39
Hill, Major Gen. D. H., battle of Malvern Hill, 42; and Lee, 61; a new corps formed, 62; at Fredericksburg, 63; Grant advances on Hill's line, 68, 69
Holstein River, 11th Ga. crossed to Morristown, 68
Hood, Gen. John B., fighting in West, 62
Hooker, Gen. Joseph, had begun grand offensive, 61; Lee planned to offset Hooker attack on Richmond, 62, 63
Horses, Army, 2, 8, 9, 23, 24, 25, 26, 29; Thompson horse, 55
Hospitals, general, 12, 24; Culpeper, 17; First Ga., 17; No. 2 Ga., 16, 17, 18, 19; Winchester, 5
Huts (Confederate), 21, 22

Indian House, 11th Ga. on picket duty behind, 15

Jackson, Anna, wife of Stonewall, 12
Jackson, Gen. Thomas, "Stonewall," mentioned x, 2, 4, 7, 12, 38, 39, 43, 46, 50; "Stonewall" name gained, 6; religion in camp, 11; "Uncle Stone," 51, 52, 54; nicknames, 54; Thompson's description of, 55; death, 59, 62, 64
James River, 29, 31, 32, 39, 42, 43, 60, 61, 71
Johnston, Gen. Joseph E., in Shenandoah, 2; evacuated Winchester, 3; ordered Bee and Bartow to go to aid of Confederacy, 6; Jeff Davis met Johnston and other generals, 7; and Quaker guns, 32; relinquished command to G. W. Smith, 37

Kelly, Bud (Thompson neighbor), 55
Kentucky, Morgan tearing up, 52
Knapsacks, 3, 7, 29, 35
Knoxville, Tenn., Longstreet headed toward, 68

Ladies, 1, 8, 22, 44
Laseter, William T., mentioned, xi, xii; article, 59, 63, 65
Lee, Gen. Robert E., xii, 32, 37, 38, 42, 44, 47, 60, 61, 62, 63, 64, 65, 68, 74, 93
Leesburg, Va., battle at, 16; Leesburg on Potomac, 50; barefooted men remained behind, 46
Lincoln, Abraham, disagreed with Scott, 1; pen to change destiny of many, 31; and McClellan, 39; and Lee, 62
Litter bearers (Confederate), 69
Little River turnpike, 11th Ga., 16
Longstreet, General James, foot cavalry, x; Corps 50 (Hagerstown), 59, 60; mentioned, 5, 44, 51, 61, 62, 63, 64, 65, 66, 67, 68, 69
Louisiana Zouaves, receiving commands in French, 37
Lowe, T. S. C., and observation balloons, 31

# INDEX

Luffman, Lt. Col. Wm., left behind in hut, 14; met enemy near Mechanicsville, 36; left troops, 40; wounded, 45

Magruder, "Prince" John B., "Quaker" guns, 32, 33; south of the Chickahominy, 38
Malvern Hill, 39, 42, 43
Manassas, 1, 2, 3, 4, 5, 6, 7, 12, 17, 19, 25, 49
Martinsburg, Va., 11th at, 51
Maryland, campaign, 46, 47, 50, 51, 52, 62
Masons & Skinner's Horse Fairier, 24, 25
McBean, Dr. David S., 2nd Ga. Hospt., 19
McClellan, Gen. George B., 26, 29, 31, 34, 38, 39, 42, 43
McDaniel, Henry Dickerson, First Lt., ix, 23, 28, 59, 66, 92
McDowell's troops, 5, 6
Meade, Gen. George G., 64, 67
Means, Dr. (Confederate surgeon), 12
Mechanicsville, 36, 39
Medicines, 12, 13, 17
Messenger (horse), 19, 24, 25
Militiamen (see also troops and volunteers), 1
Missionary Ridge, 68
Mitchell's Ford, 4
*Monitor* (ironclad), 31
Monocacy River, 46
Monroe, Ga., 23, 24, 25, 46
Montpelier (home of Pres. James Madison), 27
Morgan, John, 52
Morgan's Cavalry, 68
Morristown, Confederates in winter quarters, 68
Morrow, Lt. J. W., 64
Mules, 23, 31, 55

Nansemond River, 60
Negroes (Union troops), 70
New Kent County, Va., 35
Ninth Georgia Regiment, 14, 36, 63
Norfolk, Va., Jeff Davis in, 30; U. S. Naval Yard, 32
North Carolina, Longstreet on foraging trip to, 60

North Carolinians, at battle of Yorktown, 36
Nunnally, Josiah E. (Joe), First Sgt., Co. H, 11th Ga., ix, xi, 48, 49
Nunnally, Capt. Matthew Talbot, Co. H, 11th Ga., mentioned ix, xii, 20, 21, 29, 90; letter, 8, 13, 16, 21, 27, 29, 30, 34, 42, 47, 63
Nutt's Hill, Capt. Stokes and his men occupying, 14

Orange Court House, Capt. Nunnally and Co. H, 27; James Thompson writing from camp, 28; James Thompson left for battle of Fredericksburg, 30

Paris, Va., 11th Ga. rested, 3
Patterson, Gen. Robert, deception used by Johnston and Jackson, 2
Pemberton, Gen. John C., at Vicksburg, 62
Pennsylvania, Confederates among Unionists, 52; Lee moved into, 62
Petersburg, Va., Longstreet at, 60; Grant and Lee, 71; Field's Division, loaded on cars for, 72
Piedmont, Va., Co. H marched to, 3; took passage for Manassas, 4
Pine Branch, Co. H pitched tents, 13
Pontoon Bridge (near Farmville), Confederates, 73
Pope, Gen. John (Culpeper, Va.), 47
Porter's Corps, 39
Postage, lack of, 41, 44
Potomac River, 16, 17, 27, 28, 46, 50, 51, 59, 61, 65
Pounds, Numan (DeKalb County, Ga.), neighbor of Thompson family, 23, 35
Preston, Richard M., First Corp., Co. H, ix
Prisoners, 7, 17, 35, 50, 71

Railroads (see also box cars), 4, 5, 6, 25, 28, 36, 52, 69
Rapidan River, made bridges of wagons, 27; enemy at Racoon Ford, 47; Lee's defensive position behind, 67

Rappahannock River, 11th Ga. encountered enemy, 48; Federals left in night, 58; detached Longstreets' troops from, 60
Religion, in Stonewall's camp, 9, 10, 11, 28; and Thompson, 27, 28
Republicans (in Georgia), 22
Rice Station, Longstreet doubles picket lines, 72
Richardson, William C., fifer, Co. H, ix
Richmond, Va., 1, 2, 4, 5, 16, 28, 29, 30, 31, 32, 34, 35, 36, 37, 39, 60, 71; Seven Days' battle, 42, 70
*Richmond* (ship), 60
Roads, general condition, 26, 29, 31; New Meadow Bridge, 36; Darby Town, 71; Fairfax, 45
Roanoke, Va., 25

Savage Station, Magruder attacked enemy, 39
Savannah, Ga., Co. H expected to be there April 1862, 30, 31
Scott, Gen. Winfield, 1
Secession flags, used at Bull Run to deceive Confederates, 1
Seddon, James, Secretary of War, 60
Seven Pines Battlefield, 37
Seventh Georgia Regiment, 33, 36
Sharpsburg, Va., Confederates fell back, 50; Ewell's men to march to, 62
Sheats, James N., Third corp., Co. H, ix
Shenandoah Valley, Joe Johnston against Federals, 2; 11th Georgia, 3; Kirby Smith came from valley to Henry House Hill, 6; Jackson brought men from valley to Mechanicsville, 38, 39; Co. H ordered to, 59; Retreat by Longstreet through, 67
Shepardstown, Va., Co. H waded Potomac at, 51
Sherman, General William T., 68, 71
*Shreveport Journal* (excerpts from), xii, 59, 61, 67
Sickness, 12
Singleton, John (Thompson's friend), 5

Singleton, William (Thompson's friend), 5
Sixteenth Georgia Regiment (?), 33
Smith Alexander H., second corp., Co. H, ix
Smith, Gustavus W., at Centreville, 7; Johnston relinquishes command to, 37
Smith, Kirby, commanded part of Johnston's men, 6
Songs, mentioned, 3, 8; "Maryland, My Maryland," 47
South Carolina, Charleston, 67
Springfield Muskets, 33
Spruill, John (Thompson's friend), 22, 23
Stable (Confederate), 26
Stephens, Alexander H, visited Ga. Hospitals in Va., 18
Stokes, Capt., commanded Confederates at Nutt's Hill, 14
Stone Bridge, over Bull Run, 5; Major Nathan P. Evans holding, 6
Strasburg, Va., 11th Ga. from Manassas to, 2, 3; Confederates in valley, 59
Strawberry hill, 11th Ga. camped, 36
Stuart's Cavalry, picket at Kelly's Ford, 67
Sudley Springs, Federals moving via, 6
Suffolk, Union forces, 60
Sullivan, Mrs. Martha S. (owner of Nunnally letter), xii
Surrender at Appomatox, 74
Susquehanna River, 62

Tents (Confederate), lack of, 7; illness in, 8; hospital tents, 12; chimneys in, 21; sufficiency of, 26; protection of, 58;
Thompson, Bob (Thompson family Negro), 26
Thompson, Elizabeth (sister of James), 9, 22, 27, 51
Thompson, Harriet (sister of James), 9, 22, 27, 51
Thompson, Henry (brother of James), 9
Thompson, James Thomas mentioned, vii, xi, xii, 7, 8, 9, 25,

# INDEX

31, 42; letters, 4, 5, 11, 12, 16, 20, 21, 27, 28, 38, 43, 46, 51, 52, 53, 55
Thompson, John (brother of James), 9
Thompson, Lucinda Hardman (mother of James), 9, 24, 27, 40
Thompson, Mary Jane (sister of James), 9, 22, 27, 51, 91
Thompson, Riley (brother of James), 9
Thompson, Thomas (father of James), 9, 10, 16, 20, 22, 24, 30
Thompson, William (brother of James), 9
Thompson, Wyatt (brother of James), 9
Thoroughfare Gap, Co. H at, 48
Tiger Rifleman (New Orleans), killed, 21
Tobacco, 22, 58
Tombs, Maj. Gen. Robert, 36

Union, armies, 1, 2, 5, 6, 52; batteries, 6; soldiers, 38, 39, 44, 60
United Confederate Veterans, xi

Vicksburg, Gen. Pemberton at, 62
*Virginia Magazine of History and Biography;* Thompson letters, xi
Volunteers (see also militiamen and volunteers), 1

Wagons, 3, 29, 31, 52, 54, 65
Walnut Grove, Ga., 24, 25
Walton Infantry (Georgia), 23, 40
Warren, Kittrell J., x, xi, 2, 6, 12, 13, 14, 22, 26, 32, 36, 37, 44
Warrenton Pike, McDowell at, 1, 5; Evans on guard at Stone Bridge, 6; Federals fled in panic from Bull Run, 7
Washington, D. C., 1, 2, 7, 28, 62
Water, x, 12, 33
Weather, x, 6, 7, 12, 13, 14, 15, 16, 20, 21, 23, 26, 30, 33, 36, 48, 57, 60, 65, 68

Wells, Carl W. (owner of Thompson letters), vii
Wells, Mary Jane Thompson (see Thompson)
West Point, ix, 6, 35
Whiskey, 10, 67
White Oak Swamp, McClellan moved through, 39
Wilderness, 11th Ga. going to Gen. Lee, 68
Williamsburg, Va., battle, 34
Williamsport, Va., Ewell and one column via, 62; Confederate wagon trains, 65
Wiley, William (Billy), wounded at Gettysburg, 64
Winchester, Va., Co. H marched to, x; Johnston assembled forces near, 2; evacuated, prep. Manassas battle, 3, 4; tents left at, 7; 11th Ga. fell back to, 51; cooking 3 days rations, 52; Co. H camp near, 55
Winder's Hill, Co. H detailed for picket duty, 13
Wrightsville, Pa., 62
Wood, Thomas G., drummer, Co. H, ix
Woodall, Powell (friend of James Thompson), 5
Wright's Legion (DeKalb men), 39
Wynn's Mill, 11th Ga. marched toward, 32

Yankees, xi, 5, 6, 13, 14, 17, 19, 22, 25, 28, 31, 33, 35, 42, 43, 45, 48, 51, 52, 55, 57, 61, 65
Yorktown Va., Co. H embarked on James River schooner for, 29; Confederates not needed at, 30; McClellan moving toward, 31; Johnston retreated from, 34, 35; Howell Cobb there, 36
Young's Mill, 11th Ga. bivouacked at, 45

www.ingramcontent.com/pod-product-compliance
Lightning Source LLC
Chambersburg PA
CBHW030146240426
**43672CB00005B/294**